Upcycle Your Congregation

Creative Ideas for
Transforming Faith Communities

Sarah Lammert, Editor

Skinner House Books
Boston

www.skinnerhouse.org

Printed in the United States

Cover design by Kathryn Sky-Peck
Text design by Suzanne Morgan

print ISBN: 978-1-55896-815-8
eBook ISBN: 978-1-55896-816-5

6 5 4 3 2 1
21 20 19 18

Library of Congress Cataloging-in-Publication Data

Names: Lammert, Sarah, editor.
Title: Upcycle your congregation : creative ideas for transforming faith
    communities / Sarah Lammert, editor.
Description: Boston : Skinner House Books, [2018] | Includes bibliographical
    references.
Identifiers: LCCN 2017046350 (print) | LCCN 2017059540 (ebook) | ISBN
    9781558968165 | ISBN 9781558968158 (pbk. : alk. paper)
Subjects: LCSH: Church renewal. | Unitarian Universalist Association.
Classification: LCC BV600.3 (ebook) | LCC BV600.3 .U63 2018 (print) | DDC
    253/.39132--dc23
LC record available at https://lccn.loc.gov/2017046350

We gratefully acknowledge permission to reprint the following: "As Unitarian Universalists we believe…" by Anthony Makar, reprinted by permission of author; an adaptation of Deuteronomy 6:10–12 by Peter Raible, reprinted by permission of author's estate.

Contents

Introduction

For a holiday gift two years ago, my teenage daughter gave her younger cousin an Altoids tin. "That must be a joke," I thought to myself, but then her cousin opened the tin to reveal a felt teddy bear bed inside. The blankets were glued in, but my niece could remove the bear and then tuck it back in. She shrieked with delight.

It turns out that my daughter had made this adorable toy in her "Upcycling" class at school. Since then, she has come home with a table she made from an old TV tray, hair clips glammed up with baubles, and other, more abstract art objects she made from things like old computer discs, broken jewelry, and odd pieces of hardware.

Watching this parade of recycled, cast-off objects transformed into beautiful, fun, creative new forms, I found myself pondering the quandary of church these days. So many churches are treading water or in decline, yet the yearning for spiritual practice, inter-generational community, and connecting soul work with justice making are very much alive. Could we upcycle the main ingredients of congregations and transform them into something relevant, creative, and new?

This book is for real-life leaders of brick-and-mortar congregations, both professional and volunteer. It is for the committed, budget-stressed, busy, stretched leaders who love the church and can also clearly see its challenges. This book is not about changing everything in head-spinning ways, but being inspired to experiment in the service of vitality. It is about taking the ingredients you have at hand—the buildings, the worship life, the mission, the people, and the programs that make up your religious community —and creating new possibility.

These authors are people like you—real-life congregational and religious leaders who have found a way to make new wine from old wineskins, attracting new growth and vitality where things had gotten a little dim and dusty. In one case, it was a simple as flipping worship and coffee hour—inviting people to attend coffee hour as the main event on Sunday. In other examples, new vitality came when the leaders became laser-focused on a mission and started telling a new story about themselves that made them the heroes of their own story rather than bystanders helpless to effect change.

The world has always called for spiritual communities to bring forth the full weight of their power to the struggle for a more just, more compassionate, more loving way of being. These days, this call turns to a shout as economic and racial disparities, environmental concerns, and systemic violence take on greater intensity and call for a stronger response. Many people are lonely, dispirited, and in need of transformational hope. Now is the time for congregations to take some risks in the service of innovation and new life.

Have a large, old building? Upcycle it. The First Parish Church in Taunton, Massachusetts, did just that, and it now hosts a social services agency that provides emergency food, case management, and medical care for poor and homeless folks of the city. Have a commitment to antiracism? Julica Hermann de la Fuente has some ideas from twenty years in social justice education and her work with the Fahs Collaborative for ways to build the Beloved Community by putting faith formation, not identity politics, at the center of this work. Learn from Tandy Scheffler, a master-level credential religious educator and minister, about how embracing multigenerational community brings new life. How about mashing up some music and adding a little Motown to your hymn singing? Could you use some fresh ideas for your outreach program to new members? These examples and more are brought to life in this volume.

You don't have to start from scratch to bring vitality to your congregation. You don't have to take it all on at once. There are simple, yet profound ways you can use the riches you already have around you to create fun, relevance, vitality, and beauty in your religious community. Enjoy the journey.

Sarah Lammert

The New Revised Standard Version of Our Story

VANESSA RUSH SOUTHERN

The differences between the two congregations I have served as a called minister have been as stark as one could expect for two institutions planted within the same faith family. However, despite their differences, each congregation had a core similarity: each had, at its heart, a story that described its past and animated its future. That story, almost more than anything else, was the key to its health and survival. That story was also subject to the age-old religious art of redaction.

"Congregational storyteller" almost never shows up in any minister's job description. But words like "visioning" and the expectation that the minister will keep holding up the mission in front of the congregation will make it into those descriptions. However, what those words and phrases and expectations actually require of us is never clear or explicit. How does one *cast a vision* after all? Is it like casting a line into a river, trying to catch a fish—a little bait, a good spot, a lot of waiting? Or is it like casting a hit show—auditioning possibilities until something clicks?

To create a vision—weaving something that lures and electrifies people out of mere words and images and that speaks to its history and current circumstances—is an art. To wed it to the community's sense of itself in such a way that the whole body will be willing to lean hard into adversity in order to live into that shared dream is magic. Only a storyteller can do this kind of work.

So, a key piece of leadership is the role of congregational story-teller. Central to that role is the nuanced and vital work of learning how to rework the story a congregation tells about itself—something we might call "re-storying" a congregation's life. I once asked a valued associate for advice at a time when a congregation I served was not being faithful. This colleague said that part of our job, at certain times, is to keep a congregation's best self in safekeeping until it is ready to reclaim it. Often, when we "re-story" a congregation, we find a way to restore its best self and a mission worthy of that self.

We do this work by asking, "Is this the *only* story we can tell?" and looking with new eyes at the people before us for the untold story. We redact the details, add ones someone chose to leave out long ago, eliminate others that seem extraneous to the larger point, and create the New Revised Standard Version of the gospel of who the people before us are and who they are called by Spirit to be. It will all be true, because there are many versions of the truth, but our version should be the one that invites them to unleash their own brand of magic and fierce love into our waiting world.

Caroline Webb, an economist and former partner at McKinsey & Company, reminds us in her book *How to Have a Good Day*, that you and I only see part of reality at any one time. Our deliberate mind, she says, has a limited capacity to process information. Our subconscious, somehow knowing this, helps by filtering out a great deal of the information from the world around us so that it can leave the deliberate mind with just enough information to do its job. It turns out, though, that the subconscious mind takes clues from the conscious mind about what sorts of things it should favor as it does this work of sifting through information.

All of this makes sense, right? How often, when you are jay-walking at rush hour, have you noticed the architectural details of the street you are on? How often, in an intense meeting, have you noticed what people in the room are wearing or the sounds in the hallway outside the room? Do we think about our email or how tired we are when we're in the middle of watching a really good movie? No. Our brains sort for what our rational mind decides is most important at that moment, and in masterful, unobtrusive ways.

All this means that you and I see and register much less information than what comes at us in any given moment—a small fraction—and that we see mostly what we want, intend, or expect to see. Despite saying to ourselves that we are open-minded people, you and I are far less open to new, challenging, and life-upending information and experiences than we like to think we are. Studies drive the point home.

In one study at Harvard's Visual Attention Lab, Webb recounts, a group of radiologists were given real lung scans and told to look for abnormalities. In the last image they were given, however, a picture of a gorilla was pasted inside the lung. Amazingly, 83 percent of the doctors did not see the animal, even though it was almost fifty times the size of the nodules the radiologists were scanning to find and despite the fact that eye-tracking devices showed that the doctors' eyes indeed passed over that part of the image. As Webb summarizes it in *How to Have a Good Day*, "Their brains simply didn't consciously register the ape. In other words: because they weren't actually looking for it, they didn't see it."

Our filtering out of much of the world—and doing so based on preexisting biases or interests—affects a great deal of what we do and how we do it. It explains, for instance, why we feel there are some people we "just can't win" with; people who determinedly filter out the good they could see in us and register only the bad. And it explains why there are people who probably can never win with us. It explains how believers worldwide see proof everywhere of the God they already believe in. And how this baffles their detractors, who see instead mountains of evidence against that same God. This phenomenon of human processing of information and the world also helps explain the strength and persistence of stories.

In her novel *The Palace of Illusions*, Chitra Banerjee Divakaruni illustrates this phenomenon in the words of one her characters, who said,

Suddenly I was tired and heartsick. I thought, I shouldn't have chosen this story. Every time I spoke it, it embedded itself deeper into my brother's flesh, for a story gains power with the retelling. It deepened his belief in the inevitability of a destiny he might have otherwise sidestepped.

All congregations come with a story, sometimes more than one. Often we hear the story soon after we enter the building. There can be a sense of lore around it—something well practiced and honed over time into a tale that is increasingly both mythical and compelling. The story often resonates through the version of the congregation's history that its people tell. Ideally, it echoes in the mission and vision statements they hold themselves accountable to.

Usually, the members have learned particular anecdotes that highlight key themes of the story and anchor it in the collective imagination. A healthy church has healthy anecdotes—tales of love, courage, and laughter, and of the good, long journeys across the wilderness places. Churches with unhealthy patterns, on the other hand, tell other kinds of anecdotes—ones that encourage distrust, fear, a sense of embattlement. When we hear the anecdotes of the second type we encounter our first clue that the bigger story being told is one that Larry Peers, director of the Center for Pastoral Excellence, calls a "problem-centered story."

A problem-centered story, as you might have guessed, is one that a community (or individual) tells about itself that has a problem or a barrier, seemingly unmovable, that magically reappears in the lives of its people. The congregation's job too easily becomes (officially or unofficially) looking for that problem and reconfirming how this barrier is a cross to bear. This obstacle also bars the congregation from any great work in the world and makes its story one of endurance and suffering. The barrier can be anything. Often it is money or ministers, people's bad behavior, or the limits of size. It is frequently a story of a world theologically at odds with the congregation, which is often a version of the story of (terminal) uniqueness—a kind of curse of its own (secretly prideful) specialness. There are probably hundreds of versions of the barrier, but in all cases, they get in the way of a congregation being liberated to serve with love, power, and joy. The identified problem becomes an excuse to be small in heart, mission, or size; congregations somehow get stuck in it.

The role of anyone in leadership has to be to dismantle barriers to service, to heart, to mission. God/spirit/life didn't make us permanently incapacitated for service. So, stories that say or imply we are debilitated for such things have to be innately suspect. Somewhere, even in the most dispirited congregations, something bigger than their small story is working in ways that create instances of greatness, grace, beauty, and the whispers of real calling. Leaders, ministerial or lay, are the ones whose hearts incline them (or who have cultivated the gift to listen for) the strains of a call above the congregational mantra of problems. Or to hear the strains of a new call when that is what is needed.

The work of re-storying a congregation begins, then, with a leader looking for the signs of life, grace, or call beyond the mantra of problems and barriers and then weaving them into a new story, credible and real. Credible, because it is grounded in truth and reality; real, because it speaks to the possibilities of the present moment.

The first church I served was located in the heart of Washington, D.C., just a mile from the White House. If you could have levitated and looked south down the street, you would have seen the president turning on his night-light as you walked home from your evening meetings at church. This church had been built in the late 1920s as the Cathedral of Universalism, once the fifth-largest denomination in America.

In its time, the church was prestigious. The minister's weekly sermons were summarized in the Monday edition of the *Washington Post*. The congregation was home to ambassadors and senators and good citizens from all walks of life. Its members were lit up with a commitment to the Universalist message of unconditional divine love and the challenge to be disciples of that love.

Over time, as most of us know, the denomination started to shrink. In 1961, the merger with the Unitarians took place, though few, if any, members at this church welcomed that marriage. As they saw it, Universalism's power was not so much doubled as halved. Indeed, the Universalists' assets were sold off: schools, colleges, seminaries, camps, and conference centers were liquidated to provide cash for a new merged denomination. And the Unitarians, drawn disproportionately from the powered elite of the nation, disproportionately called the shots. Of the first three presidents of the merged denomination, all came from the Unitarian side.

In April 1968, something more locally devastating happened: the city of Washington lit up in the flames of despair and rage. Like Chicago, Baltimore, Detroit, and other cities, the nation's capital erupted in violence and riots the night Martin Luther King Jr. was assassinated. As a result, Universalist National Memorial Church, once surrounded by vital neighborhoods, was now flanked by empty townhouses and burned-out avenues, as people left and businesses shut down or relocated outside the city center.

This church, however, didn't leave. At some point, it covered its stained-glass windows with plexiglass to protect them from rocks or worse. No doubt there were other changes in the life of the community as a result of what the city was facing. But the congregation voted to stay where it was. It stayed committed to the city and to being a presence there. It stayed committed to its role as a place holder, a keeper of the flame of Universalism against all the tides of change. It was a stubborn act of faithfulness in the face of the erosion of the city and the perceived erosion of the denomination it loved.

I heard this central story when I first met this congregation and was called as its associate minister. The story echoed again and again in the choices and self-conception of the institution. The significant theme was "protecting a legacy." The people in this community were preservers of legacies—of Universalism, of a vision of Washington, D.C. They held a lot in keeping until the world was ready to reclaim it. They were a kind of "holy remnant," in the way the Bible describes it.

As in many historic churches, however, I also sensed a fear of losing ground. The congregation was already small after years of attrition. People were concerned that if we loosened any of the moorings to the past, the rest of what we loved might also be lost. This concern often focused on parts of worship, particularly the 1899 Universalist Declaration of Faith that we said weekly. More than once, a member told me that this piece of liturgy had to remain unchanged, because if we removed or altered it, what held the church together would be gone and so would we.

One result of this core identity and the fear connected to it was that the Universalist message had not been allowed to breathe much. Progressive Christianity outside our walls was asking much more radical questions than we were about what God's love, unleashed, meant, and about what forms church life could take to express that love.

A dig-in-your-heels, batten-down-the-hatches response to adversity is not unusual. It is a natural way to weather a storm. But at some point, we have to open the hatches we have battened down to see whether the storm has passed; eventually the time comes to rebuild.

In some ways, when the Universalist National Memorial Church decided to call an associate minister, it felt like an unbolting of the hatches. The former senior minister, Bill Fox, had come back part-time, after the negotiated resignation of the previous minister, to steady the ship. Hiring another full-time staff person to assist him was definitely a risk for this church of only ninety active members. The members had voted consciously to overstaff the church in an attempt to jumpstart a new chapter of growth and stability. The decision meant spending down a significant part of the church's reserves.

Against the story that had predominated—the one about weathering adversity—this decision raised the question of the role that risk played in the congregation's story, past, present, and future. There was risk enshrined in the very building in which they gathered.

* * *

The Universalist National Memorial Church is an architectural gem. The building was designed by Francis Richmond Allen and Charles Collens, the same architects who designed Riverside Church in New York City and oversaw the reconstruction of the Cloisters in New York, to name only two of their many noteworthy accomplishments. Money for this project, the denomination's cathedral, was raised nationally. National conferences would be held there. The local congregation would pay the staff and operating expenses, but the denomination would help build the cathedral that everyone would share ownership and take pride in.

All went forward according to plan. Universalists who sent donations received symbolic bricks to thank them for their gifts to the construction efforts. Children sent their pennies from around the country to build the stone baptismal font. However, in 1929, before all the money had been collected, and right before the construction was to begin, the stock market crashed. Gifts shrank and pledges disappeared in the margin calls of the market.

There are so many ways to tell this part of the story. Was the building a tomb that enshrined the story of the bad-luck church? There is no doubt that the effects of the crash were huge. Part of the property on which the originally planned church and meeting spaces were to be built was sold off to help offset construction costs. Faux plasterwork replaced some of what was originally supposed to be stone in the sanctuary. What was ultimately built was a shadow of this congregation's original dreams and plans for it. Was that the story?

Or was there another?

Because that building did get built. Against odds and obstacles, it was built. A monument of a building with a Tiffany cross mosaic in its nave and stunning Chartres-blue glass windows. Its sanctuary is an unusual combination of majestic and intimate. And in the space behind the altar, etched in stone, are the words from 1 John 4: "He that dwelleth in Love, dwelleth in God and God in Him." For sure, the translation is outdated in its gendered pronoun for the divine, but still, it captured what mattered most to these people, which is love, basic and uncompromisable.

People who were clear about what mattered made this building possible. They faced down the biggest financial crisis in American history in service of it. This story about their building was the one worth telling, not the bad luck that changed the plans but the grit and fierce faithfulness in what they accomplished against the odds, and a love they etched into stone as a gift for generations to come.

* * *

Once the theme of risk started to emerge as relevant, and particularly important to remember at this time in the life of the congregation, then the central job of leadership became to hold up stories of risk wherever we found them—both in the congregation's past and in its present life. We wanted to keep opening up the hatches. The time to remain protective had passed, and we needed to see a way forward. This way, however, had to be connected to who the congregation already was and who its people had always been.

So we looked for the stories everywhere. We called out the biblical stories that talked of risk. We talked about all the history of Universalism that was about risk. We pointed out what we saw happening in the lives of our people outside of church and how they served the world with Universalist love at their work and in their communities in courageous ways. We celebrated and deepened great work that they had begun, like outreach that the congregation had started years before with Whitman-Walker Clinic, a local nonprofit that specialized in HIV care.

Simultaneously, we achieved and named victories everywhere we could in our congregation's life and work: from planting flowers in the yard to show the neighborhood we were alive and well to forming a local theater group that made the church a destination for local young professionals looking for a creative outlet. We held a one-year anniversary service in honor of Matthew Shepard, the young man who had been tied and left to die on a fence in Laramie,

Wyoming, ostensibly for being gay. We offered the community a place to mourn the dangerously unwelcoming world many in our neighborhood knew all too well. We celebrated the first holy union for a same-sex couple that was covered in the wedding pages of the *Washington Post*.

We, in leadership, intentionally looked at the congregation through the lens of risk-taking, creative, Universalist love. We looked for it coming more and more alive among us. And soon the rest of the congregation looked for it and started to see it, too.

As Caroline Webb and Larry Peers both pointed out, what we look for, we often find. Indeed, we were increasingly finding evidence of this risk-taking love as our story. The next natural step was that people found themselves living more and more deeply into that story, individually and together. This is what Jim Collins, the American business consultant, calls the "flywheel effect."

In his book *Good to Great*, Collins talks about the momentum organizations can gather. "Point to tangible accomplishments," he writes, "however incremental at first—and show how these steps fit into the context of an overall concept that will work. When you do this in such a way that people see and *feel* the buildup of momentum, they will line up with enthusiasm." Collins points out that people want to be part of something that they believe matters and that can achieve measurable results. Show them that the church's story is a real story—both true and truly taking root—and the momentum and the magic begin.

It is that "flywheel" effect that we leaders are deputized to activate.

* * *

In all the churches I have served, re-storying has felt like some of the most central work I have had to do. The story we tell in each community we serve or are a part of will be different, indigenous to that place and people. However, the work behind re-storying is always crucial, and we go about it similarly, no matter where we are.

The work starts with a detective's mind. It begins with diving deeply into the congregation's history and spending hours pawing through archives for the much-told and untold events. We look for the dramatic twists and turns, for people and historic conversations that strike us as important, as unusual, as miraculous. That same detective's spirit has us seek out longtime and new members, listening for all the signs of the holy, for some guiding spirit of the place in the past and the present. Eventually, themes emerge, and not just the ones we think are there.

The job of the congregational storytellers involves intentionally not choosing the stories that put problems at the center. Some leaders like those stories—whether they are conscious of it or not—because problem-centered stories get them off the hook. A church with a problem at the center will never soar; its leaders will never need to learn how to fly. Everyone in those places stays safely on the ground. But leadership is not about keeping you and others grounded, not in that sense. It is about call, that way of being that is grounded only in trust and that asks us constantly to step into the unknown and serve.

So, we have to exorcise the problem-centered stories. We can tell the problem parts of the stories and sometimes should, but not as the end of the story. Instead, we recast them as the opportunities for learning that they were, for the ways they taught us persistence and strength or maybe pushed us back into important insights. What did losing half our members in our division over the Vietnam War teach us about community? That we should avoid politics or that we must always be prepared and practiced in how to weather difference together, in love? Dig for life, wisdom, and hope in the stories' twists and setbacks. Tell that version.

Finally, see the victories and accomplishments of spirit everywhere you look. Look for them so that you will see them. Then celebrate them. Hold up the good, not just some distant ideal, but wherever it shows up. Tie what happens every day back to the big picture of who the congregation is and is ever more called to be.

In the end, our job is to choose the version of the congregation's story that is about life and where God/spirit/love is calling the community now. To do this job, we reweave threadbare narratives with vibrant materials found in their attics and current life together. To do this job, we teach the congregation a new song, as leaders have before us—songs familiar enough that the members recognize the tune, but with notes that ring true to their ever-reborn world. This weaving, this song writing, this re-storying are the perennial work of the leader—a vision-casting bard of the forever upcycling congregation, finding and telling the New Revised Standard Version of its gospel tale. Then, helping the community live into that story together, happily, purposefully, faithfully ever after.

Making It Matter

CHRISTANA WILLE McKNIGHT

My first contact with the First Parish Church in Taunton, Massachusetts, came through a Facebook message. I had told the district executive that I was looking for a ministry in the area, and a few days later, a man who identified himself as the board president sent a message saying he would be interested in talking with me. The board members had seen my work in my previous congregation and were intrigued. I was feeling sore from a recent ministry that I deemed unsuccessful, but held on to the hope that somewhere there might be a church where my skills could be useful and we could grow together. The Facebook message startled me, as I imagined a church with a 375-year history would be conventional in every possible way.

When we had our first conversation, the board president was clear about the lay of the land. The building was enormous—more than fifty thousand square feet. The downtown neighborhood was working class, the poorest section of a city in which more than 50 percent of its students received free or reduced-price lunch. The congregation, once a standard bearer in New England, had shrunk to perhaps thirty people on the books, with Sunday morning attendance often in the single digits. The endowment was getting smaller by the day. The congregation wanted to do something different. It didn't want the church to close with a whimper, silently shutting the doors the day that no one came on Sunday morning. It was ready to try anything that would bring it life.

The board of trustees and I met for the first time in the Sunday school room. At that time, the board included the majority of the members. We talked about our ideas. I told them what I thought was necessary, just at first glance, to give the church a chance at surviving. Specifically, the congregation needed to embrace the modern era wholeheartedly and create a church for the twenty-first century, even knowing that none of us had any idea what that would look like. They agreed, and were eager to explore any possibility. We signed a contract three weeks later.

We talked a lot that night and, in the following weeks, about what it might feel like to revitalize a church that used to be enormous, both in terms of attendance and influence. We sat in a church that had been built when churches were the center of city life. It had been built "to honor God forever" as a soaring neo-Gothic stone cathedral, standing out from the white New England meetinghouses that dotted the neighboring town landscapes. Taunton had changed over the years, and the Yankee mill owners and manufacturing giants were long gone, replaced by Portuguese and Cape Verdean immigrants, and a struggling infrastructure. An arsonist had set fire to the city hall across the street from the church several years before; it was still not repaired. The city was struggling along with the church, and optimism was on thin ground.

First Parish had huge liabilities, as anyone who visited there could see, and it was not situated in a traditionally Unitarian Universalist setting. The surrounding area was thick with Portuguese Catholics and other subgroups who generally didn't flock to a liberal Protestant church. A few of my mentors tried to dissuade me from working with the church, pointing out the obvious challenges—a tiny congregation, barely visible infrastructure, no committees at all except the board of trustees. The building—huge, beautiful, historic—was as much a burden as a gift. And yet.

"What we do needs to matter." Those words became the guiding light for me and the board of trustees in those first few days, weeks, and months. The people of First Parish—though small in number—blew me away with their honesty and their hearts. They were willing to try any number of crazy ideas, as long as they knew that, at the end of the day, their church would be transforming the lives of their neighbors and friends, of people in need, and of themselves. They were, and still are (though today we have a totally different group of people), completely committed to the idea of Unitarian Universalism above all else, committed to the theology and understanding that we are placed here on this earth to love each other and that we must do that with all the days we have in our lives. They are people who love each other and whose love stretches beyond those whom they have known for years and reaches to those they have not yet met.

After the first two years of my ministry in Taunton, we made a concerted effort to connect with the community beyond our walls in new ways, including working with the Matthew 25:40 Mission. During my travels in the city, I had met a group of volunteers who regularly gathered food and clothing from the community and distributed them in an abandoned grocery store parking lot once a week, handing them out to anyone who wanted them. I had heard about their efforts and invited their leaders to a meeting at First Parish. I told them how our congregation wanted to be involved with helping those in need and asked if there was anything we could do. They responded immediately: "We need an office. Some place to hand out bags to people that isn't the trunk of a car." We at First Parish rearranged a few things, and within six weeks, the Matthew 25:40 Mission was rebooted in our congregation. The volunteers joined First Parish and began to spread the news about their good work, inviting people in and helping them with paperwork, handing out food and warm clothing to anyone in need. Soon the lines outside the small office we had given the Matthew 25:40 Mission began to snake down the hallway, and we were becoming the first referral for the police when they were trying to get someone into housing or otherwise off the streets.

Then we knew we needed to grow our ability to minister to more people. As the leaves started to turn, our thoughts went to those who would be living in the snow in just a few short months.

There was an old room in the basement of the church that had flooded the year before. The room was a mess after the flood, and I was terrified to think about what it might take to make that space habitable again. But, as with so many things, the vision of the church, the words of our leaders propel our actions: "What we do needs to matter."

One day, when our volunteers had served thirty people from the tiny office on the second floor, I screwed up my courage and went down to that basement room, Stevenson Hall. I sniffed the air, which was still musty. The floor was layered with ancient glue, and some of the lights didn't work. Yet there it was—a huge empty room. A place where people could gather. A place that could help energize our growing congregation, bring us together, and help us reach out to the community. With a determination to be brave, I went upstairs to our administrator.

"Do you think there's a way to get that glue off of the floor downstairs?"

She laughed. "There's a way to do everything. It's just a question of how and who and how much it costs."

Google searches brought up a few options, none of which worked. Then one of our maintenance workers came up with the answer: a hard-core, diamond-tipped sander. We rented the drum sander, and the guys who used it were led by (I am both proud and dismayed to say) my husband.

This was just the beginning. Next we asked the volunteers working in the Matthew 25:40 Mission, "What do you think about the idea of expanding?" We talked about a variety of possibilities and were reminded again about the question around the edges of almost every conversation with those who were in need, especially those who were homeless: Where can you go to be accepted? There are agencies to help, but when you are on the margins of society, darting under bridges to back alleys, struggling with addiction or PTSD, there are few who love you as you are. We decided we wanted to be one of those few places where everyone was accepted and valued. We wanted to extend the mission that we had on Sunday mornings so that every day at First Parish would be a place where people were not just welcomed if they happened to wander in, but a place that they knew was there for them. We wanted to become a center for gathering where people could further live out the mission statement of our congregation—to inspire, connect, and serve, every day. The Matthew 25:40 Mission began to grow.

We sanded, painted, and cleaned. As the old, flooded room began to transform, we began to dream. Donations of couches and chairs, shelves for food, magazines, and paint poured in. Volunteers —people who had never before stepped into our church, or any church for that matter—came to move dry goods and clean off a fine layer of dust from the sanding. Three months after that first time I had wandered into our previously flooded basement, we held the grand opening for the Matthew 25:40 Mission and Out-reach Center for Those in Need. The mayor spoke, the community gathered, and we received citations from the state legislature. In the first year that the Outreach Center was open, we served more than a thousand people who came for emergency food support, case management, or medical care or a place to just rest. We became an internship site for the University of Massachusetts–Dartmouth Nursing School and began to offer foot care for our guests, many of whom walk miles each day. We offered behavioral health ser-vices through a local agency, as well as STD and STI testing, and formed partnerships with local veterans' groups.

Yet, in spite of all of the amazing partnerships that we forged and continue to form, and all the resources that we help make available to people, what I hear the most from our guests and oth-ers in the community is about the character of our people: "The Matthew Mission is where they are kind to you. That is where they treat you good. You'll be safe there." Some people come every morning, some don't stay more than a half an hour but come to get their coffee, and some sit for a few minutes and now have a place that they can call a little piece of home.

As we built the mission and continued to expand our dreams and visions, the First Parish Church began to matter in all kinds of new and amazing ways. We began to be a touchstone in the community, a place that people knew they could depend on, and most of all, where everyone knew they would be treated with respect. With the expansion of the Matthew 25:40 Mission, what we did as a church began to matter in a whole new way.

The mission has become our link with the community, but Sunday morning worship is at the heart of First Parish Church in Taunton. The congregation and I were true to our words when I started here; we have largely revamped the Sunday morning worship, from singing a new and wide variety of songs to creating a different kind of prayer and including visuals in the worship. Guests from the mission often join us on Sunday morning, noticeable because of the layers of clothing that they wear or because they ask if they can take coffee-hour cookies back to their campsites.

About three years ago, one visitor told me affirmatively how much we have changed. She said to me, "Your church is loud." At the time, I'd been the minister at First Parish for a few years. Our Sunday morning attendance had grown steadily, though the congregation was still incredibly dwarfed in the five-thousand-square-foot sanctuary that seats more than seven hundred people comfortably. We had roped off the back pews to force people to sit together or at least within shouting distance of each other. The ceilings soar above us in worship, and we looked on the wall to the projected lyrics of the modern songs that we sang and the unison chalice lighting we shared together each week. The people who had been coming were enthusiastic but not always certain what "church" was all about. Their average age was about forty-one; the woman who had commented to me after worship was older than that, though not by much.

"I'm sorry? Were the speakers up too loud? I can talk to our sound tech about it . . . ," I responded.

"No, it's not the speakers. This church is just loud. People talked before worship. They clapped during the songs and after the solo. There are so many *children*. The only silence is during prayer. When I came here years ago, we were quiet during church.

That was what church was about. We were quiet and respectful and behaved. People knew what to do."

I spoke slowly, to make sure I was saying what I intended to say. "You're right, it is different. This church doesn't look like it used to, and I imagine it must be hard to come after being away for so many years and see it looking so different from what you expected. What's happening here though is that our church is living. Those noises you talk about probably are loud, but they are part of who we are. If people didn't feel comfortable talking here before worship, they wouldn't have a chance to greet new people before church starts. They wouldn't have a chance to visit with their friends or make new ones. That's what our community looks like today."

"It's different."

"Yes. It's different."

She looked at me for a moment and then asked, "Is this what all churches are doing now? I mean, are there any quiet ones or is this just what church looks like?"

I laughed warmly, and she smiled at me. I said, "There are as many kinds of churches, both Unitarian Universalist and otherwise, as you can imagine. No two churches are the same, though lots of them share similar characteristics. You're right that this one is louder than some. We have more kids, and they are part of our worship. We encourage connection, both on Sunday mornings and other times. We want to be a growing community, so that will probably be different than places that aren't working with that as a specific goal."

She looked away.

"It's okay if this doesn't feel comfortable for you right now," I assured her, as gently as I could. "You can give it some thought or come back another time, or try going to a different church and see if that's a better fit for you. I'm sure there are churches that are quieter."

She looked for a long time at the light from the Tiffany stained-glass window shining on the pews around us, and then over to the electronic drum kit we use most Sunday mornings. "This church is old and new at the same time" she said flatly. "I don't know what to think about it."

I haven't seen that particular woman since that Sunday. I think of her often, especially when the congregation laughs a lot during my sermon or when clapping breaks out spontaneously and loudly after a musical piece. Churches have changed over the years, and I think about what religious and faith community is all about. Are we of this world? Should our rituals and traditions transcend time and space, continuing on, even as the world around us changes? I tried to think about what a church service would be like for me without chalice lighting and I failed. In my world, spiritual community and the symbol of the chalice are all intertwined, working together and with each other to create communities all around the country that feel like mine. This might have been what it was like for this woman to come back to her home church after decades away—to a place in the same physical location but where the way that "church" used to be isn't practiced any more. Adapting to the world around us, retiring old traditions, and adopting what feels authentic to people today are important parts of ministry. And yet, with those adaptations there is a loss. That loss is important, and it needs to be held and valued. And yet. . . .

What we do needs to matter.

Some things about churches and congregational life are as old as creation and will always be part of what it means to be human. Gathering with others. Prayer in some form. Connection. Caring. Remembering our dead and celebrating new life. Laughter. Grief. These are inherent to the human condition and will always be a part of who we are. But what form these inherent components of life take—if we connect in a field as we pick the yearly crop or on Facebook as we wait in line in the grocery store—may not matter as much as we think it does.

The world looks different today than it did fifty, thirty, or even ten years ago. The way that we experience community has changed, and in order to fulfill our potential as institutions of faith, hope, and reflection, we too must change. This does not mean that we lose our values or who we are theologically. But it does mean that the world will develop, and we have the choice of developing with it or not. Our congregations can keep exemplifying the values that were highlighted in churches thirty or forty years ago—the values of being quiet, and the traditions of separating children from worship, the idea that the church of the poor and the church of the rich were not the same places. We could do that. But, today, our values are different. What I hear from my congregation is that we value authenticity. We value the ability to connect with new people because we don't know all that many and want to meet more. We value being with people who understand why the plight of the homeless makes us sad, and in a place where we can work every day to make the world a better place.

Of course, it looks and feels different than it used to. And there is still, as I suspect there always will be in ministry, much more work to do. But today, we are doing so many things that matter, and because of that, our church, along with so many others, is creating a new kind of hope, a new kind of Unitarian Universalism. Built on where we have come from, we are finding new ways to matter and to meet the needs of our hungry world. The mission can guide us to new ways to matter, to transform, and to connect that we have not yet dreamed of. As we often say here at First Parish, with faith, all things are possible.

It is an old story, in a way. The story of a place that used to matter and that once held the central lines of a community. But just because a place mattered once doesn't mean it will matter today or in the future. Part of our job as people of faith is to make sure that as the world changes, the way we interact changes as we see and work with it. Our churches are not a community away from the world but, rather, a community rooted in the places and times that we live in, with the people who are there with us. What we do needs to matter.

Generations Together

TANDY SCHEFFLER

I had an epiphany.

It was 2002, and I was in my fifth year as a religious educator at Oak Ridge Unitarian Universalist Church. I was attending the Renaissance Module "Worship for All Ages." We were doing a guided meditation to recall an early memory of worship. In my mind, I was a little girl, back in the church of my childhood. I was sitting in the pew, crowded close together with my parents, grandmother, and three younger siblings. I saw my little brother's plaid pants and swinging legs, my sisters' white lace-edged socks and patent leather shoes. I saw the adults' hands resting in their laps or holding mine. My father's calloused palms, my mother's wedding rings. My grandmother and I playing her secret-message hand-squeeze game. Her first two squeezes meant "Love me?" My two squeezes back replied, "Mmm hmm." Her next two squeezes asked, "How much?" This I answered by squeezing her hand as hard as I could. During the meditation, I recalled nothing of the content of any worship service. But I vividly remember the profound feeling of belonging, the deep knowing that my family, near or far, living or dead, would always be with me. It was a connection that transcended time and space. I felt myself rooted in love.

The Vision

I returned to my work as a religious educator with a new vision, beckoning like the North Star: *families worshipping together.*

As in most Unitarian Universalist churches, religious education for children and youth had always taken place during the worship service. Children attended the first few minutes of worship, then were sent off to their classes. The adults were accustomed to a rather cerebral service, free of the distractions of children. I had no idea how to get from this deeply entrenched norm to my vision of all the generations together in worship, with, as the luminary religious educator Sophia Fahs once said, "the children in our very midst."

I look back now, after years of experience and education, and can identify this as an adaptive challenge—a matter of gradual systemic change, requiring patience and nonanxious leadership. It involved years of laying the groundwork, growing in understanding, building conflict management skills, and earning trust. Around the time of my epiphany, the church called a new, young minister, Jake B. Morrill. Jake embraces change. He is a leader who encourages other leaders to follow their passions, as long as those passions support the vision, mission, and goals of the church. Families worshipping together was not a particular passion of Jake's, but he was able to appreciate it as one of mine. Over our years of working together, we have come to value the ways our visions and work styles complement each other. We have a working relationship built on trust and respect.

I have had the benefit of working with a very healthy, high-functioning religious education committee that grew as I grew. We held annual weekend visioning retreats that made space for deep conversations about the purposes of religious education. These conversations informed our work with children, youth, and families.

Over the next eight years, my calling to religious education and to ministry continued to deepen. The congregation and minister generously supported my professional development and continuing education. I developed a strong network of colleagues who shared my passion for working in Unitarian Universalist congregations. In 2007, I became a credentialed religious educator, master level. And in 2014, I completed a master's of divinity degree. I was ordained by my congregation and called as its minister of faith formation.

During these years of growth, my North Star—*families worshipping together*—became a binary star system. I became just as passionate about religious education for all ages as I was about worship for all ages. Jake enthusiastically supported this expanded vision for Sunday mornings.

A Family-Friendly Second Service

Our church had been slowly growing from pastoral to program size—that is, crossing the 150-member threshold. Our Sunday service became so crowded that, in 2008, we started having two Sunday morning services. This was a perfect opportunity to have one service intentionally family friendly. The 9:30 "traditional service," with religious education classes during the service, was the same as before. The second service, at 11:00, was our "celebration service," with everyone in the entire service, featuring contemporary music (guitars and drums) and a shorter message. We offered only nursery and preschool care during the celebration service, encouraging all ages to worship together. Our hope was that families would come to the 9:30 service, during which their children would attend their classes; then the family would stay and worship together in the 11:00 service. The vast majority of families did bring their children for religious education during the 9:30 service. A few of these families chose to stay around for the second hour and worship together in the celebration service. The celebration service became our lab for experimenting, learning how to do worship that was more participatory and engaging for all ages, and "putting the children in our very midst."

Faith Formation Hour

In 2010, the religious education committee had its own epiphany: that Sunday worship is foundational to religious education, not a peripheral add-on. At that meeting, the committee made a firm decision, something akin to drawing a line in the sand. The members declared they would no longer volunteer their time and talent to a religious education program that met during a worship service. They sent a letter to the minister conveying their deeply held conviction that children belonged "in our very midst" in worship and their intention to only support religious education that met at a separate time.

Although open to change, Jake was understandably taken aback at being handed what felt like an ultimatum. To his credit, he moved past this and supported the change. We also replaced the term *religious education* with *faith formation* and *committee* with *team*.

In 2010, the church embarked on a three-hour Sunday format with the goal of a dedicated faith formation hour between the services. We also switched the order of the two services:

9:00   Celebration Service. Family friendly. Children
        stay in the whole service.
10:00   Faith Formation Hour for all ages.
11:15   Traditional Service. Young children sung out
        after fifteen minutes.

We were well on the way to fulfilling the two visions: families worshipping together and faith formation for all ages.

During that first year of adding a faith formation hour for all ages, we built the airplane while we flew it. Jake and I had agreed that adding faith formation hour to Sunday mornings was enough change for one year, so the traditional service remained unchanged, including singing the children out after the first fifteen minutes. The question of what to do with the children for the last forty-five minutes of the second service became mine to figure out. I decided that I would lead forty-five minutes of "children's worship" in our largest classroom space. Young children would be the worshippers, and older youth could choose either to stay in the traditional service or to come out with the children to assist me with the children's worship. I scheduled the younger children's parents to take a turn assisting with the children's worship every couple months.

I look back now on children's worship as a time to teach children and, to a lesser extent, their parents, how to worship. Over time, I was able to delegate responsibility for leading the children's worship. When I took a five-month sabbatical two years later, the children's worship was deeply engrained enough to be led entirely by laypeople.

Our faith formation groups for children and youth were well established and ready to go, with a strong team of leaders. Faith formation for adults was another matter. We had only one established adult discussion group, "Reflections," which met after the service to reflect on the sermon topic. I devoted considerable hours to planning and recruiting leaders for two new weekly adult groups—one for parents and one for newcomers.

This new faith formation hour between the services was not without its problems and detractors. Some longtime members lamented the loss of the beloved coffee hour for relaxed socializing all together, without competing activities. And we lacked adequate meeting space for three adult groups. The only spaces we could utilize—the main foyer, a corner of the social hall, and my office—were either very noisy or very cramped. Faith formation hour, sandwiched between two services, got squeezed from both sides and was really more like fifty minutes. Everyone felt rushed.

I put out some fires, practiced a good bit of active listening, and repeatedly put forward a nonanxious presence. The minister and I were a united front on the changes we had introduced. And a core group of church leaders supported and championed what we were doing. Attendance for adult faith formation groups that first year was enough to make all three groups viable. We made it through the first year without major problems. It was a year of many extra hours for me.

One Blended Service

The following year, we decided to go back to one service instead of two. Attendance at the early celebration service had peaked at around thirty, short of the goal of fifty we had said was needed for viability and to make it worth all the effort that went into the service. And everyone missed the feeling of being one congregation worshipping together.

As we prepared to begin the church year in August with one service, Jake led a very intentional process to bring as many people as possible into a conversation about the style of the single service. We held an evening of conversation about worship. We began with a covenant to listen first, to try to understand one another, and to say "I" (feel) rather than "a lot of us" or "some people." We asked people to share their reasons for coming to worship and their favorite parts of the service. We aimed to capture big-picture ideas that Jake would use to guide him in designing the single blended worship service. One of the most polarizing factors was music—contemporary versus traditional. These discussions were lively and revealing. For example, one elder said she really disliked seeing the drum set on the chancel, even though it was not used in the traditional service she always attended. It didn't fit with her idea of how the chancel ought to look—dignified and simple. Another church elder said she had felt that same way at first and for the same reason. But then she served on a committee with the drummer. As she got to know him, she came to feel entirely differently about the drums. They now reminded her of the young man she knew, liked, and appreciated.

Reflective conversations like this helped people understand worship as a shared experience of a diverse congregation in beloved community. We went forward with a single blended Sunday service. We have the contemporary band some Sundays, the choir and pianist on others, and occasionally both. We sing a wide variety of songs and hymns. The drum set has stayed on the chancel.

During the four years since then, the blended service has gradually leaned more toward a contemporary service style. We have added a couple of high-energy gathering songs to the beginning of the service. More of the congregational songs are easier to sing than the word-dense traditional hymns.

Historically, Unitarian Universalist worship services have engaged mainly one sense—hearing. We listen to the spoken word and to music. These days, we appreciate that individuals take in information in many different ways, including all five senses. We also do so through activity—by doing, not just by listening and thinking. We enrich the worship experience when we find ways to engage all five senses and ways to remain active and creative during the service. We have added lots of multisensory, participatory elements to the "altar building" segment of the service. What began simply as a time for candle lighting has become a time to move around and engage with a number of different stations in different areas of the sanctuary or to select items to bring back to contemplate or be creative with during the service. We have a place to write joys and concerns to share in the prayer. We provide blank greeting cards to draw and color, later to be mailed to congregants in need. We have a ceramic pool of water, with stones, flowers, or other seasonal natural objects to take for contemplation or to release into the water. We have two candle-lighting altars. We offer various tactile materials, such as Play-Doh and pipe cleaners, with which to be quietly creative.

The message is shorter, around fifteen minutes. The worship context involves experimentation and something for everyone. The congregation has increasingly embraced worship as something the community actively creates together, rather than as a presentation passively received. Admittedly, this does not appeal equally to everyone. Some feel a sense of loss, missing the high-church traditions of the past, including the music. Newcomers, however, tend to embrace this more participatory worship with enthusiasm.

Along with these gradual changes to the style of worship, we have gradually lengthened the time the children are in the service by a few minutes every year. First, we kept them in the service for altar building; then for the prayer that follows it; then for the offering, which they can help collect. Today, children in kindergarten through fifth grade attend an average of forty minutes of the service—everything except the message, closing hymn, and benediction. When they are sung out, they go to "children's time" for the remaining twenty minutes, where they have a snack and supervised play.

About every two months, we mix all ages together, either for the entire service, during faith formation hour, or both. During faith formation hour, the whole congregation gathers together after worship for some shared endeavor or celebration, followed by lunch. Most recently, we washed all the interior windows of the church and then celebrated the accomplishment with pizza.

Deus Ex Machina

In the middle of all our experimentation and gradual shifts, we received a totally unexpected and game-changing gift. Just as we were ready for a capital campaign to renovate the original sixty-year-old section of the building, a commercial developer made a generous offer for our property. The offer would allow us to relocate to a bigger lot in a desirable location and to build a bigger and brand-new facility. The congregation voted to accept the offer. The year that followed was intense. The mixed and raw emotions around the impending move and demolition of our old building permeated all of church life.

We worked with an architect to design a sanctuary suited to our emerging style of participatory all-age worship, with more flexibility in seating arrangements and more room for moving around during worship. We also got more and larger spaces for faith formation groups. We moved into our new building in 2014. We would probably have continued in the direction we were headed without the gift of a new building, but our new space has certainly made the shifts we were making easier. Adult faith formation groups, in particular, are flourishing in the new building.

Vision Fulfilled!

In August 2016, just after Ingathering Sunday, the traditional UU water communion service, I really felt we were "there"—that my vision from fourteen years before had been fulfilled.

All ages were in the entire service. In the sanctuary, pews faced the center. There were about eight different activity or sensory stations, some in the center of the room and some around the perimeter. There were every-Sunday altar building stations. Additional stations for this annual celebration included four themed tables with vessels to receive the summer's waters, colored-paper slips for writing a phrase about the source of the water, and a ritual cleansing hand-blessing ritual performed by a family. Youth hosted the tables where water was received and participated in telling the story.

The ingathering service was followed by a fifteen-minute transition time before faith formation hour, the start-up session of groups for the new church year. There were five weekly faith formation options for adults that day:

- "Faith Forward," an open group for newcomers, in the back of the sanctuary. Refreshments provided. Several church leaders welcomed the newcomers and introduced them to the church.
- "Reflections" in the library, a discussion group reflecting on the service.
- "Nomadic Yoga" in the outside pavilion. ("Nomadic" because they vary their location depending on weather or other factors.)
- "Circle of Trust," a closed covenant group, sharing deeply on the monthly theme of joy.

- "EMBERS" (Earth-Mindfulness Based on Earth Religions), our pagan group.

Adults were also free to skip the faith formation experience, and some simply hung out and enjoyed coffee in the social hall.

That Sunday during faith formation hour, I walked through the building to check on all groups. I poked my head into the nursery. There, I counted eight babies and toddlers happily playing on the floor. Scattered among them were eight or nine adults. They too looked quite content. The parents of our babies and toddlers, along with some adults who are not actively parenting, love hanging out there and choose to be in the nursery week after week. The nursery is a multigenerational ministry. Our littlest ones are surrounded by adults who know and love them and who also know and love each other. It's a fine example of "putting the children in our very midst."

If the babies could talk, they might say, "Would you just look at these adorable adults? Why, here they sit, in our very midst!"

May it be so!

Beloved Community

JULICA HERMANN de la FUENTE

I can only answer the question "What am I to do?" if I can answer the prior question "Of what story or stories do I find myself a part?"

—Alasdair MacIntyre

Eight years ago, the Unitarian Church of Harrisburg, Pennsylvania, moved into an inner city church building. At an appreciation dinner a few years later, an elder in the African-American community stood up and said, "You know, I have been wondering. I have been trying to figure out what is different about you people. What is going on here, and why are you here, and why do you stay here?" The participants at the dinner held their collective breath. Here it comes, they thought to themselves. She continued, "You know, I think you're here because, unlike most white people, you're not afraid of us."

Their minister at the time, Howard N. Dana, continues the story:

And in that moment, we all sighed, and smiled, because she got it half right. We were totally scared to be there, but we went anyway. What we actually managed to do was get over our fear and meet folks where they were, and be kind, and be as generous as we could. And even through all the mistakes that we made, and all the clumsiness, the recognition that we were still there was really wonderful.

Today, this midsize congregation of approximately 320 members is serving breakfast twice a month to approximately 400 folks in the community. Dana went on,

> And it just kept growing, and it kept growing, and it kept growing; more and more folks wanted to volunteer. And it was that meeting of one another that made it work. People showed up both to provide the breakfast, and people showed up to partake in the breakfast. Then we started to see those lines be blurred. The people in the kitchen would go eat with the folks who had shown up for breakfast, and the people who had shown up for breakfast would then the next week want to show up and help out in the kitchen. And so it became this community in a way that if somebody hadn't said, "Yeah, okay, this is now our responsibility, we're going to do it as well as we can do it, and see how it works out." If nobody had said that, if we hadn't shown up, that relationship wouldn't have been created.

How do we do that? How do we help Unitarian Universalist congregations build bridges with local communities of color and become effective in their antiracism work?

The Unitarian Universalist Association is in the midst of a crisis as it struggles with the white supremacy embedded in its systems; leaders from the Black Lives UU Collective called for a teach-in about white supremacy in all of our congregations, and for renewed efforts to address the issue of racism both within and without. The response has been complex and prolific. To those of us who have been involved in antiracism work in our denomination, the conversation is neither new nor surprising. However, many ministerial colleagues, religious professionals, and lay leaders are engaging in these efforts for the first time, or for the first time in a long time.

Conversations about race and racism have not been so central in our denomination since the black empowerment/white power controversy of the late 1960s and early 1970s. Even before the recent events within our association, the Black Lives Matter movement that started with the acquittal of Trayvon Martin's killer; the antiracism protests and militaristic response by the police in Ferguson, Baltimore, and other cities; a growing awareness within our denomination and the larger white society of the school-to-prison pipeline; and the media storm surrounding the abuse of power by police and the killing of so many of our African-American siblings have all contributed to a heightened degree of urgency. They have intensified our commitment to closing the gap, as Mark Morrison-Reed puts it in *The Selma Awakening*, between "Unitarian Universalism's espoused values and our values in practice" regarding racial justice. Layered on top of this rising awareness and commitment is Donald Trump's election, his current xenophobic immigration policies, and the spike in hate crimes against people of color around the country. Compounded with recent events in our association, including the resignation of four of the top leaders in the Unitarian Universalist Association and the Ministers Association, the conversation about antiracism is more heated, more urgent, and more pertinent than ever. Unitarian Universalist congregations across the country and the leaders within them are hungry for tools, resources, and solutions.

My own involvement in antiracism efforts in Unitarian Universalist congregations is rather new. As a result of my studies at Meadville Lombard Theological School, I started collaborating with Professor of Religious Education Mark Hicks in the Beloved Conversations project in 2014. Over the past few years, I have traveled around the country, working with lay leaders and clergy, leading the opening retreat of the Beloved Conversations program, and generally coaching folks on their struggles to become better allies and create more effective antiracist congregations. This work has confirmed my previous experiences in higher education and as a social justice educator over the past two decades. Using the metaphor of upcycling, and drawing from my own experience creating upcycled sweaters, I know that the work is to trust that something new and beautiful will emerge from the pieces of former garments. We have some very good cloth to work with; there are some challenges that we are still carrying from past patterns that we need to remove in order to create a new garment that is effective moving forward.

Three Levels of Work

In order for Unitarian Universalist congregations to be effective in racial justice work, we need to understand and work on racial justice at three different levels:

- First is the *individual work* that we all need to do to understand our own social location and the impact of our social identities. Until now, many of us have approached this work as an academic and sociological exercise; this work is much more effective when we see it as one of faith formation and spiritual development.
- When we reframe antiracism education as an act of faith formation, we can immediately make a connection to our *theology*. In order to help us move collectively away from a perfectionist paralysis where we need to understand and get everything right before we spring into action, we need to cultivate an ethic of risk, as suggested by theologian Sharon Welch, and truly learn what it means to be a covenantal faith. We need to leverage our theology as a communal and public practice, not a private and individualistic one.
- Once we have engaged our own individual work and begun to articulate a theology that supports our work in community, we can shift to looking at the congregation itself as an institution that works to end

racism. The *organizational work* that we need to do in our congregations is to understand how our practices, policies, and procedures are drenched in white supremacy culture. In order to do this effectively, we need to focus on two areas: looking within the congregation at its practices and procedures and looking outside to our work with the surrounding communities and our roles and relationships with them.

Here I address only the first of these challenges and point to future opportunities in the other two areas we must engage as we become more effective in our antiracist work.

The Challenge for Individuals to Get Past Identity Politics

When I first started working as a social justice educator, I taught others the way I myself had been taught. I situated myself squarely as an immigrant, middle-class, bisexual Latina, and I used my identities and experiences to help others become more aware of their privilege and their own social location. (A few years into this work, I learned to add cisgender and temporarily able-bodied to that list of identities.) There is absolutely nothing wrong with that. We very much need to continue to become more aware of our own social location, of the intersection of the identities that we all carry, of the way that privilege and oppression play out in our institutions and on our bodies.

Yet, at other unconscious levels, I was working out my anger on the people I was supposed to be educating. I was taught to inhabit and leverage a space of righteousness, a holier-than-thou position that gave me (for once) the upper hand. I was taught to talk about my pain and my anger, about how outraged I was at the micro-aggressions that I experienced every day, about the many ways in which American society failed me. The meta-narrative in all of my stories was "you don't understand what it's like to be me." The goal of these educational encounters was ostensibly to create opportunities for people to wake up, to see their privilege, to recognize the ways in which they colluded with oppressive institutions. I was also looking for opportunities to validate my own experience and needs.

Some of my friends and colleagues, including other UU ministers, have described similar experiences. One referred to it as a hazing ritual, a process through which we were awakened to our privilege and also trained to bring others through the same painful process. In a recent Facebook discussion with a UU minister colleague who prefers to remain anonymous, she named the challenge this way: "The things that are really hard in my context is that we've sent a lot of people to antiracism training. People consistently come back from training as the 'antiracism police' monitoring everyone else's language and offering criticism but not actually doing very much."

Yet it is not so simple that we can discount or eliminate identity politics altogether. Although I wish we could speak from a place of identity-free neutrality, I recognize that this is a desire to minimize our differences and to universalize our experience, one that actually privileges the status quo and dominant groups. Attending to identity and noticing whose voice is or is not being heard have been important parts of our radical politics and liberation movements. They are *still* crucial parts of our work, especially at a time when the new hateful rhetoric in the public sphere is targeting many folks. My critique of identity politics is not a call to return to the former status quo; rather, it is a desire to transcend. I want to be fully immersed in what Sharon Welch, in a speech to the 2013 UUA General Assembly, called the third wave of activism and social justice, focused on action and collaboration. This third wave of activism follows, first, the commitment to and struggle for equal rights (fought for in the sixties), and, second, the "resolute claim for the complex identities and full humanity of all groups marginalized and exploited by a systemic oppression and silenced through cultural imperialism," in the eighties and nineties.

In order to achieve that third wave of action and collaboration, we first need to collectively get out of our own way. Shutting down white people in conversations about racism ("You just don't get it!") will get us nowhere. On the other hand, continuing to create safe spaces where we set the same old ground rules, tiptoeing around white fragility, and expecting people of color to do all the work by educating the white folks are also not helpful.

At the same time that we recognize our identities and our voices, we need to identify an end game that is larger than any one of our own personal experiences. We do this by working on it in our faith communities. By creating a larger container that focuses on our faith formation helps us understand how these difficult conversations about racism and oppression affect both our spiritual lives and our congregations.

An intentional commitment to being the folks who bend the arc toward justice requires that those of us who identify as white move past our feelings of fear, inadequacy, guilt, and shame and find ways to step into effective action that supports the efforts of our leaders of color. It requires that those of us in the global majority notice when we are doing what Starr King School for the Ministry President Rosemary Bray McNatt calls the "spiritual domestic work" of our white siblings, and what we have sacrificed in our own spiritual formation to attend to that work. Most important, we need to create new understandings that we do this work not just individually, as we work through our own challenges and educate ourselves, but in community with each other.

As we grapple with the topics of accountability, responsibility, and just basic awareness of racism, we also need to focus on the challenge of belonging. Where are the communities that help us understand the impact and experience of racism? Where are the spaces where we can collectively examine our role in the system and ways in which we can subvert the status quo? The answer is in our UU congregations. We need to engage in a collective meaning-making process: We need to look at our theologies, at the stories that we tell ourselves about why we do what we do, and who we belong to and with. As we construct the stories about what is right, what is moral, and what is just, we also need to attend to the stories that help us understand what brings us joy, satisfaction, and even pleasure. For too long, antiracism work has been tinged with guilt and shame for those of us who identify as white, and with pain, anger, and impatience for those of us in the global majority.

Once we are able to place our own experiences and identity development in the context of larger stories and communities, we can then also bring our attention to the way that racism operates in those systems. We can step beyond the strictly personal and begin to analyze the institutional. This work is difficult and crucial. Unless we see the way the status quo operates in all of our institutions, including our churches, we will continue to be more a part of the problem than the solution.

Upcycling Our Antiracist Religious Education

Jubilee and Journey Toward Wholeness, the antiracism programs offered in UU congregations over the past two decades, have provided important opportunities for many of us to wake up to our social location and privilege. However, they have also been fertile ground for the dynamics of identity politics I have described previously.

Two relatively new approaches have appeared on the UU antiracism education scene: the program Who Are Our Neighbors, and the Beloved Conversations curriculum. Both programs, in different ways, help us reach beyond a focus on identity politics and toward an understanding of antiracism education as a faith formation practice. They bring a developmental lens to our work: they are grounded in the understanding that we are all on a continuum of growth and learning, ever evolving in our grasp of both the individual and institutional implications of racism.

Who Are Our Neighbors is a program initiated by the UU Ministers Association and now carried on by regional staff from the Unitarian Universalist Association. Who Are Our Neighbors helps us identify our location on the Intercultural Development Continuum, a model that both raises our awareness about our relationship to other cultures and invites us to continue to develop our intercultural competency. This model is grounded in the idea that intercultural competency develops over time. We all enter and see the world from a monocultural perspective, and through different experiences, we are slowly challenged to change our worldview and make room for others.

We are all, white and people of color, in the process of becoming. We are all in the process of understanding how to be more interculturally competent with each other. When engaged in conversations about antiracism, it's helpful to remember that some folks at the table are approaching this work from a position of minimization or denial. Although frustrating at that moment, I am more patient and compassionate as I hear people describe their understanding of the world from a vastly different perspective from mine. The framework challenges me to my own personal growth, rather than setting me up as the expert person of color, here to educate the well-intentioned white folks in my congregation.

Beloved Conversations is a curriculum of the Fahs Collaborative, housed at Meadville Lombard Theological School. Mark Hicks created it to support the antiracism education efforts at First Unitarian Church of Portland, Oregon; it has since grown into a program offered around the country, with more than a hundred congregations participating at the time of this writing. This eight-week curriculum creates a powerful way for Unitarian Universalists to increase their awareness of their role and participation in the status quo and their opportunities for more fruitful antiracist efforts.

Beloved Conversations, a great example of upcycling, uses familiar exercises that have been used successfully to help people see their social location. Privilege Walks and the process of caucusing in racial groups are examples. What is different are the questions that frame these exercises. Folks are invited to look at the spiritual costs and the meaning they have made of their social location. In the tradition of small-group ministry at its best, this program invites people to look deeply and honestly at their life experiences, and to grapple with the theological implications of their life choices with respect to race and ethnicity. It assumes that both white folks and people of color need to do this work, rather than situating people of color in an expert position.

Beloved Conversations also looks at the congregation itself as a site for change. Based on the understanding that every single institution is steeped in a culture that privileges white supremacy, this program challenges us to see that membership in a liberal church does not exempt us from this pattern. Our UU congregations, like every other institution in this country, have standard operating procedures and unspoken agreements that maintain the racial status quo. The way we worship, the way we run meetings, and the way we treat ministers and religious professionals of color all point to the work that we still need to do.

Talking about race and ethnicity is scary. Looking at the ways that we are involved and complicit with the status quo is scary. Many of us have spent time and energy trying to demonstrate that we are not racist. What we need now are containers and spaces where we can begin with the assumption that we are all, in fact, racist and part of racist institutions. We are all part of the problem, and therefore part of the solution.

This is our work. To speak the unspeakable. To create appropriate containers where we can share the pain, the frustration, and the challenges of dealing with racism. But these containers also need to inspire us to take more risks, to focus on "brave spaces" rather than "safe spaces"—a distinction clarified by Brian Arao and Kristi Clemens in *The Art of Effective Facilitation*—to help us recharge our batteries so that we can bring a loving and critical eye to the many institutions we belong to (including our UU congregations), and slowly but surely change them to reflect our values.

Some people believe that the Promised Land is where every single congregation reflects the rainbow of skin tones in our society. Although it is certainly important to ensure that our congregations are a welcoming space, it is not productive to simply focus on "the hues in the pews." Rather, we should consider whether our congregations are courageous spaces in which to talk about racism. Do we think and talk about racism from a theological perspective? Do we make meaning together about the impact of racism in our lives? Do we leverage our churches to serve as allies in our local communities? Do we take leadership from those communities and show up humbly and with a willingness to listen and follow? What stories do we tell about ourselves and our role in ending racism? When we worship together, do we find many ways to connect with spirit and with each other? Is antiracism a part of our congregational mission and vision? Are our congregations collaborating in local community efforts with organizations that serve people of color? When we are able to thoughtfully and affirmatively answer these questions, we will be able to say with joy and confidence that Unitarian Universalism is at the forefront of antiracist efforts, consciously building the Beloved Community. May it be so.

Worship Alive

KEN BELDON AND LEE PACZULLA

"I thought to myself, 'Okay, . . . so this may be a cult.'"

These were the words our newly minted worship leader, Jessica, spoke to the congregation one Sunday morning last September. After our opening song block—three alt-rock, pop, or bluesy gospel-style tunes performed by our nine-piece band—Jessica's extemporaneous introduction and welcome, and the lighting of the chalice, she stood at the center of the stage and began to tell her story of discovering WellSprings Congregation. She found out about it the same way most people do nowadays: through Google.

She said, "Before I came to WellSprings, I investigated you guys online. To tell the truth, I was looking for something like a Yelp review, but no such luck, so I poured through the website, curious to see what you had to say about yourselves . . . and I don't know if you all know this, but there's a big banner image across the top of the site . . . with a bunch of adults, standing around blowing bubbles." Then, in Jessica's droll way, with a pause for effect, "I wasn't sure how I felt about that."

Our congregation laughed. Our congregation laughs a lot. We laugh in worship, we laugh in meetings, and we laugh together in small groups. We laughed along with Jessica's story because we could relate. In the Philadelphia suburbs—and particularly in status-conscious, achievement-focused Chester County, consistently ranked as the wealthiest county in our state—appearing responsible and appropriate at all times can seem important. It's important to appear (if you'll pardon our language) as if we have our shit together. The broader American can-do culture, which places like Chester County are thought to exemplify, encourages us to seriousness of purpose, hard work, and excellence in all we do—if not perfection. Critics are everywhere. We should engage in leisure, where appropriate, in a modest and measured way. It's a culture that, our congregation recognizes, can keep us living in boxes, not willing to let ourselves experience all that there is and could be. Not willing to let ourselves experience the fullness of being in our bodies, for the short time we have here on earth—to truly experience the fullness of being alive.

Our Unitarian Universalist faith is not immune to this rationalistic, perfectionist culture. As UUs, we claim to approach the world with hearts that trust. Our own Peter Mayer sings that "everything is holy now"—that all things are pregnant with sacred potential, that God is not limited by forms we can imagine, and that truth and meaning unfurl before our eyes as we live. We say that revelation is forever unsealed, co-created in community, and ongoing to the edges of existence and beyond. Yet, sometimes our actions belie our teachings. There are taboos within many of our congregations, including what is new, emerging, and youthful. We can label such expressions "cute" or "trendy," too silly for the seriousness of worship in our often difficult, challenging world. We consign these things to "children's church," separate from the adult experience of worship. We may fear a sense of vulnerability that arises with pre-rational ways of being. We know the very real dangers this vulnerability carries, and yet at the same time, we crave opportunities to experience it. We know that connecting with each other in the fullness of who we are—shit, silliness, and all—helps to heal us from this culture that demands conformity to a box, or a role, or an image. At WellSprings, we notice that the things children do appeal to something pre-rational in us. Blowing bubbles, modeling with Play-Doh, dancing eagerly in worship, exploring the world through tales of cartoon characters and superheroes are all things that we have integrated into our congregation's worship life.

Worship services at WellSprings might be appropriately described as "contemporary." The word offers a useful shorthand, as it conjures up images of drum sets; headset mics; doughnuts at coffee hour; tattooed pastors who walk the stage in jeans, shirts untucked—all of which you'll find on a typical Sunday morning here. Our choice of worship style, however, is not a tactic for appealing to the young and hip. Chasing hipness, we know, is addictive, a loser's game. There will always be some community out there that's more hip, more relevant, and more cutting edge than we are.

The choices we make in worship at WellSprings are a living embodiment of the "holy now" theology we commit ourselves to—the theology that says the stories that bear meaning in our lives come from everywhere and anywhere. We upcycle at Well-Springs by renewing and extending a holy-now theology, which, in many congregations, ground to a halt because of excessive references to cultural touchstones of the boomer generation, NPR programming, and the occasional Rumi quote. We set our holy-now theology to work on the current means of communication, to create a more richly diverse community, and to cultivate an accessible experience of communion within our congregation. Breaking down barriers between church culture and real-life culture allows us to more fully engage our faith beyond our doors, but it's also a deeply rooted theological practice that helps us recognize the divine imprint in the music we stream, the stories we watch, and the social media we post and share. It lines up perfectly with one of the core beliefs affirmed by our congregation: "the Burning Bush is blazing everywhere."

Most people know what a "meme" is. Richard Dawkins first introduced the term in his 1976 book *The Selfish Gene*. It is a sort of cultural gene—which may show up as an idea, style, practice, or image—that self-replicates and mutates as it spreads from person to person through social transmission. Memes on the Internet translate this phenomenon into the language of the online world: images, text, and video. Essentially, a good meme that gets shared hundreds of thousands of times on the Internet is like a giant joke everyone can be in on and can add their own flavor to, if they like.

The website CalmingManatee.com produced a set of wildly popular memes around the middle of 2013—a series of close-up photos of manatees in the wild, accompanied by comforting phrases of the kind a dear aunt might murmur to you while nuzzling your tear-stained cheek on the couch. One image caught our attention immediately at WellSprings. The text—"Don't do that to yourself. You are so loved."—is deeply relevant in a world where self-judgment and comparison run rampant, and addictions, overwork, and other harmful behaviors threaten to destroy us from the inside out. The day we used this image in worship, it felt like a bit of a risk. Yet when fleshed out with preaching and connected to the core values of our spiritual tradition, it left many of our people in tears. WellSprings has a thriving and vital addictions and recovery ministry; that morning we were talking about how we can interrupt the harmful ways whereby "hurt people hurt people." Drawing on the wisdom of Brené Brown, we encouraged folks to see how our healing can integrate our hurts without turning to harming ourselves or others when we're suffering. The calming manatees point at a transformative truth—that we all know pain, that none of us is alone, and that we can all participate in a greater, reconciling experience of loving and being loved. We integrate images such as this one that are shared online into our worship life because they do hold real power. The ones that really take off tend to tap into wide cultural currents of truth that may run deeper than we think.

This kind of cultural accessibility lies behind our decision to do those contemporary church things—like play popular music in worship and preach in everyday clothes—and it's key to how we express our holy-now theology within a WellSprings service. These practices, for us, are one more way of living out another of our congregation's core values: Sunday mornings are not about "getting religion" for one day a week. They are about motivating and sustaining our faith so that it develops throughout the week and appears in our everyday lives.

Part of the power of cultural accessibility is that it shows up in mutually reinforcing ways. Early on in our community's worship life, a new family came to visit for the first time. Their young son was slouched back in his seat—perhaps unhappy to be torn away from a morning of video games or soccer practice or reading—but he perked up significantly when he heard our band launch into a song he knew from the radio. Suddenly excited, he tugged at his mom's shirt, saying, "Mom . . . they're playing a *real* song!"

In the same way, we find that when our congregants now see one of those manatee memes, it gives them a lot more than just a chuckle. Those images carry a new resonance after church has helped to make them holy. They remind our people of our faith and the love that is available and accessible to us all. These practices require all our worship leaders, lay and ordained alike, to be constant learners—to enter into the stories and experiences around us with real humility.

Engaging with the culture that surrounds us is not a diversity strategy, though it can have the effect of bringing new people into our congregation. Instead, we find that an honest commitment to cultural accessibility naturally transforms who we are, particularly when taken to the very edges of what we know. It offers us a way of extending authentic hospitality to the world outside our church, which, of course, is where most of our people spend the vast majority of their time. Cultural accessibility, like the breath, runs in two directions. *In*, drawing on the expanse of inspirational resources all around us in our lives, helping to create vital connections between the rest of life and what happens in Sunday morning worship. And *out*, sending our people back into the world, recharged, rejuvenated, more able to recognize the holy in our midst everywhere and more able to offer #ordinarypraise for the dignity, beauty, and meaning that is all around us. This virtuous cycle, like revelation, like breath, is ongoing.

Of course, a fully alive worship experience requires more than just attention to our sources. It also requires the presence of a meaningfully growing, moving, living, and breathing community. Worship at WellSprings is intentionally crafted to welcome a wide affective range. The people who walk into UU congregations every Sunday morning are so much more than just butts in the seats, listening ears, or volunteers in a functional system. They are human beings. Loved by many; despised, isolated, or ignored by some; walking around with other people's voices ringing in their ears, anxieties and expectations firing in their nerves, a complex web of relationships tangled up within their pumping, tender, broken, and healing hearts. Our people come to us every day in the midst of emotional journeys that words can't quite speak to but that sometimes simply require a physical release.

Our rationalist Unitarian forebears viewed embodied experiences in the church with suspicion for hundreds of years, but we can't deny that our lives are made up of much more than impeccable logic and thought. There have been pointed, at times hostile, criticisms of our dominant styles of worship—"dead from the neck down," "God's frozen people." But a friendly critic of our movement, the humanistic psychologist Abraham Maslow, noted in *Religions, Values, and Peak Experiences* that a rational style of religion can make us distrustful of the earthy, emotive, and ecstatic experiences in the spiritual life. When we look askance at these authentic, even transformational expressions of spiritual life, we miss out on a significant portion of the human experience—of what it means for us to flourish.

At WellSprings, we make space for embodied experience by reflecting it first at the heart of our mission, which is taken from Walt Whitman's poem "I Sing the Body Electric"—"to be a community charged-full with the charge of the soul." Our band, worship leaders, and ministers model for the congregation how few things are off limits on Sunday mornings. Our people cry, laugh, curse, jump, dance, sing with the band, sit with the breath, take selfies, chat with their seatmates, hold hands, stretch and bend, raise their arms, bow their heads, knit, listen, hug, and play. Often all in one hour. We consciously turn toward each other in this, walking the talk of that holy-now theology to welcome a sea of constant motion that means the single, thirty-something mom with a cough, the autistic child who needs to cruise around during the service to feel safe, the shy gentleman who scurries away just before coffee hour begins—all are welcomed to be with us as they are. In all of this, of course, we are able to honor that there are different ways of learning and knowing the content of worship. Even more, we enact and place our trust in the idea that there are multiple embodied and expressive ways to know that deep belovedness expressed in our faith, that we know to be true, and that *all* of these ways of knowing—through head, hands, and heart—are good.

The great midcentury gardener of our faith, A. Powell Davies, might not have used the phrase *shit, silliness, and all* to describe what we carry into church, but he did know the power of authentic connection in a world where a host of alienating, self-preserving constraints seem to rule our days with an iron fist. "For what is church," he asked, "but dreams and hopes and yearnings? What is worship but the longing of the lonely human heart?"

We want to connect. This yearning for connection is, perhaps, the only thing that keeps congregational life going in an era where institutions are dying, denominations and seminaries hemorrhage resources by the day, and the words *organized* and *religion* are both used as dirty words—even dirtier, back to back. Communion is the promise of the church, not only the specific Christian ritual but the creative, ongoing process of pouring out our internal experiences into a wider body, where they are shared, intermingled, and reflected. Church is where the external and internal meet. Before WellSprings was launched, an earnest spiritual seeker stated plainly to us, "I'm not looking to run away from something. I'm looking to run toward something." She was seeking a spiritual community where she could connect in a space and with a place that offered the opportunity to embrace her life, others' lives, and life itself. That yearning to connect is shot through the whole of our congregational systems at WellSprings. Sunday morning worship points the way toward a whole network of more intimate ways—teams, ministries, small groups—that invite us to connect. The larger culture so often runs on our fragmentations, the judgments, fears, and all variety of oppressions that divide us within and between ourselves. To connect with compassion—this is what we offer.

The great promise of our Unitarian Universalist tradition has always been building spiritual communities where people on the margins—told that they could not use reason and conscience in church, or that their sins would keep them from the love of God forever, or that some part of who they are was fundamentally unacceptable—would find integration, healing, wholeness, and love. The highest good of our worship has never been to convey information. Today, people have access to a constant flood of information at home, online, and on their phones, all provided at a more expert level than we could ever hope to mimic. Our highest good as gathered congregations is not even to provide space for the very real magic of an intentional, open community. There are a host of other civic, social, fitness, coworking, creative, spiritual, and even consumer communities that fill this need. Many, unfortunately, are healthier, more vibrant, and better at supporting their members than the congregations of our own tradition, which are too often bound by a narrow cultural lens and a host of stale, lifeless, institutional practices. Our unique role, as living, breathing, worshipping communities, is to incarnate the holy on earth.

A grand vision, to be sure, but isn't that what the church, in all its forms across time and culture and space, has always claimed to be? Communion, in the Christian tradition, is a remembrance and an embodiment of eternal life. It is the physical consumption of imperfect symbols that point to something beyond what we know and see every day—the death, the pain, the anemic suffering of lives half-lived. When we upcycle our Unitarian and Universalist heritage in worship today, we find that what people in our context seem to crave most is life lived abundantly, outside of the boxes, images, and roles that demand our conformity in the larger social system. We crave a new way to know ourselves as beloved and worthy, which is in real conversation with the lived realities of our mundane, daily existence.

Which brings us back to Jessica's story.

You may remember that Jessica was a bit skeptical about the value of bubble blowing in worship. We don't blame her. It's a silly, childish thing to do.

She said, "I saw that picture on the website and I thought to myself, 'Am I really thinking about going to a church where they blow bubbles?' My mind was pretty blown by the fact that I was thinking about going to church at all, but adding bubbles to the mix? Wow." After expressing her relief that, on the first Sunday she came to church, no bubbles were blown, Jessica told the congregation she'd later had a change of heart:

> Two weeks ago, I came to worship, and there they were. Bubbles. Next thing you know, I'm tearing up . . . smiling so much my cheeks hurt, which makes it hard to blow bubbles, by the way. I stood there watching you all blow your bubbles. For me, the room felt so full of magic, love . . . a sense of watching people come home, watching a community coming back together, looking forward to settling into their sacred practice of being with one another. There is no Yelp review that could have prepared me for that moment. I am so happy to call myself a member of this community and, by extension of that, a fellow bubble blower. I thank you all for making a space where magic moments like that one can happen. May we all have the opportunity to experience those magic moments in our lives, with the communities that charge us full.

That worship service was our WellCome Back Sunday, a September date of ingathering after the summer. That service is our upcycled version of Water Communion. We wanted a ritual that gathered us, and also sent us. Like the breath, taking in and then releasing. Like our name, a verb—flowing, in the same way that a spring must move so it doesn't stagnate, can have life, and give life. Our bubble blowing is a renewal practice, a reminder that, whatever our age, we are not separate from the greater flow of life and love, and that to be remembered is a sacred thing. Sacred does not have to equal somber. It can be silly and joyous.

We do silly shit sometimes. We have fun. We do cute, trendy things like share memes and talk in hashtags. We play. We prioritize joy. All those things that children do—indeed, things our culture devalues in a million different ways—we don't do for the kids. But we do find that sometimes it's the kids who give the adults permission to shake their asses in the aisles, to cry without shame, to squeal with laughter at a dumb joke, and to gaze up in wonder at a sea of bubbles in the air. In the movie *Knocked Up*—which, yes, has been used as a revelatory text in our messages at WellSprings, because #everythingisholynow—Paul Rudd's character Pete muses sadly to Seth Rogen's newly blindsided dad-to-be, "Man, I wish I liked anything as much as my kids like bubbles." At WellSprings, we want people to experience life the way Pete's kids like bubbles.

There's a reason the incarnation of the holy can't be written down as a set of instructions. It's experiential, pre-rational, and transverbal; it's what the communion ritual points to, and what Jesus suggests in the Christian scriptures, when he says we will never know the kingdom of heaven or the experience of a true, beloved community "unless we become like the little children." It's what Ralph Waldo Emerson points to, when he reminds us that "we find a delight in the beauty and happiness of children that makes the heart too big for the body," taking us out of our heads, beyond what we can know with words and senses. It's nothing more and nothing less than the deep and abiding grace found in being alive—shit, silliness, and all. In worship, we get to practice being fully alive, together.

Contemporary Worship Here?

ELIZABETH NORTON

On a sparkling spring Sunday at First Parish in Concord, Massachusetts, congregants climb the front steps of the white clapboard meeting house; the minister greets them under a classic portico supported by Doric columns. They pass through double doors framed with natural wood columns and a lintel carved with the inscription, "Oak timbers from the old meeting house 1717–1900." The voice of the newly completed pipe organ, playing David Maxwell's "Meditation for the Care of the Earth" enfolds the gathering congregation of adults and children from the rear choir loft. At the front of the sanctuary, slender cherry-tree branches frame the high central pulpit. The silvery boughs with their light pink flowers draw the eye toward an image of the planet earth, which hangs on the rear wall of the chancel arch.

As the organ prelude concludes, the minister delivers a warm welcome from the pulpit. After a brief call to worship, children rise to lead the congregation in the opening hymn, Joyce Poley's "Keepers of the Earth." As a piano, electric bass, and drums begin the introduction from the front corner of the sanctuary, a group of adult singers, clad in teal-blue robes, rises from their seats under the wraparound balcony and spreads into the side aisles to help lead the congregation in song. The young voices sing, "We are blessed by every river." The adult voices answer, "Every river makes us whole." By the end of the first verse, the entire congregation is singing, led by the children's choirs and supported by the adult choir, in harmony: "For our children and our children's children we are called as keepers of the earth."

The chalice is lit to a unison response, and the congregation's social action candle is kindled with a testimony to the work of the environmental leadership team. Then the children rise again to sing a moving rendition of Natasha Bedingfield's "Love Song to the Earth," accompanied by the band. The children's message is a theatrical presentation with an intergenerational cast portraying the planets. As the children leave for religious education classes, the congregation sings a familiar refrain. After a prayer and a guided meditation led from the floor of the sanctuary, the adult choir gathers around the pulpit to sing Pete Seeger's beautiful elegy, "To My Old Brown Earth." The preacher delivers the sermon, "Every Day Is Earth Day," from the high pulpit. A brief keyboard interlude allows the preacher's words to sink in, before the congregation is invited to the social hour and a postservice sermon reflection. The preacher instructs the congregation to find the hymn number and exchange friendly greetings with one another, while the choir moves from their seats to surround and greet the congregation. Then the band and the choir call everyone to sing "For the Earth Forever Turning" with a 12/8 gospel groove. The congregation recites its unison benediction (memorized by most) and then sits to hear a brief, celebratory organ postlude.

* * *

What do we mean by "contemporary worship"? Is this it? Here, in historic Concord? Church development literature defines worship style most often by the type of music and the nature of the congregation's and choir's participation in the music. Generally, we expect contemporary worship music to use a popular style or feature "praise music." There's a soloist, a song leader, a band, maybe a choir singing backup. The congregation might join in on the chorus, reading lyrics projected on a screen. There's rarely a pipe organ (though a Hammond C3 in the band might be nice!). By this definition, worship at First Parish in Concord is not strictly contemporary, though Sunday morning worship often does include contemporary, pop, or gospel music just as often as it features classical or art music from Western and world traditions. Using music as a measure, Concord's worship style is probably best described as blended; on most Sundays, musical styles are mixed. The liturgy contains fairly traditional elements: a time of prayer and meditation, readings, two hymns, and a sermon at the center of most services.

What feels contemporary about worship in Concord is how the various elements of worship weave together to express and explore a central theme. Worship leaders combine music and liturgy in an atmosphere of innovation and experimentation that exists within and despite the very formal structure of the historic building. This ability to upcycle, to innovate within a traditional structure, has been evident at First Parish in Concord throughout its history.

The town of Concord, Massachusetts, is steeped in America's revolutionary and literary history. The dignified Greek Revival meeting house of First Parish presides over the corner of Lexington Road and Main Street, walking distance from "the rude bridge that arched the flood," in the words of Ralph Waldo Emerson in "The Concord Hymn," at the first battle of the American Revolution. Wright Tavern, the site of the first Provincial Congress and headquarters of the Minutemen, anchors one corner of the church campus. Ralph Waldo Emerson, Henry David Thoreau, Louisa May Alcott, and Nathaniel Hawthorne are buried on Authors Ridge in nearby Sleepy Hollow Cemetery. Walden Pond is just over a mile away.

Inside the meeting house, the sanctuary layout is formal and traditional. Fixed wooden pews respectfully regard an imposing central pulpit. A choir loft and a large pipe organ occupy the rear of the balcony, which extends in parallel rows of pews down the side walls of the room. The large, clear windows provide ample daylight. The walls are pale peach; the floor, painted pine. This worship space proclaims the austerity of the congregation's Puritan origin and the centrality of the word. Intellect over intuition;

formality over freedom; head over heart. And yet, the music and worship that fill this space each week are lively, inventive, soul stirring, and spirit filled.

For almost four centuries, it appears that the Concord congregation has been able to honor the tradition expressed by its buildings without being burdened by it. This has been particularly evident when it comes to music. From First Parish's founding in 1636, successive generations of ministers, musicians, and congregants have expanded upon tradition, creatively incorporating the contemporary modes and musical styles of each era into worship. Founding minister Peter Bulkeley was among the ministers of the Massachusetts Bay Colony who wrote new translations of the Hebrew Psalms that eventually became the *Bay Psalm Book* of 1637—the first English language book to be published in the New World.

The current meeting house dates back to 1901. It was raised, with amazing resilience, from the ashes of its almost-identical predecessor, which was destroyed by fire during a renovation in 1900. In all, First Parish has inhabited five meeting houses; over the generations, these buildings have been razed, rebuilt, repositioned, and redesigned. In one transition, the building was recycled by lifting it off its foundations and turning it ninety degrees. Through almost four centuries, this community has managed to upcycle its space according to the needs of the contemporary church. This is true of the present congregation as well.

The physical setup of the Concord sanctuary suggests that music is the domain of a select few: the trained choral singers and the organist. From the rear choir loft, their sound washes over the congregation, gently directing their focus toward the front of the sanctuary and the centrality of the spoken word. Until the late 1990s, the default position of the choir and musicians was in the choir loft, with the organ. Most anthems were sung a capella or with organ accompaniment. An organ accompanied all the hymns. As the choir's repertoire expanded and came to include more music that was better accompanied by piano, or movement, or drums, the choir found it necessary to sing from a position in front, near the Steinway baby grand. This prompted some creative upcycling of the sanctuary layout so that the choir could gracefully gather in the front of the church. To accomplish this, the singers sit in the first few rows of the congregation, next to the side aisles and under the balcony. They then rise and move forward to sing, surrounding the pulpit.

An acoustical quirk of the sanctuary space prompted another upcycling adjustment. Due to the angle of the balconies, it is difficult to hear the organ from the seats beneath them. When fifty strong singers stand to sing a hymn with the congregation and they can't hear the organ, they are likely to get out of sync—and even out of tune—with the accompaniment. Chaos ensues! Bringing the choir out into the aisles where they can hear the organ during congregational hymns has solved the problem. The motion of the choir has the advantage of mixing strong singers with the congregation during the hymns and increasing the confidence of the congregational singing.

By coming down from the choir loft, rising to face the congregation when they sing, and standing among the congregation during hymns, the choir's role in music making has naturally become more relational. The choir members make eye contact and share emotion directly. Organically, the culture around music and its role in worship has changed.

This new role for the choirs expanded in an unexpected way. In 2008, the reconstruction of the church's religious education wing and concurrent refinishing of the pews and the floor in the sanctuary necessitated a temporary exile from the meeting house. The relatively new Jewish congregation in town, Kerem Shalom (Vineyard of Peace), graciously welcomed the Unitarian Universalist congregation to worship in its synagogue for the summer. The two religious communities already had a history of sharing worship space: in the 1980s, before the construction of the synagogue, Kerem Shalom held services at First Parish. When the new synagogue was built at the end of the decade, the entire town celebrated its dedication with a procession accompanying the Torah from the meeting house to Kerem Shalom. Two decades later, at the time of the First Parish renovation, the Jewish congregation had just completed a beautiful new sanctuary. The Unitarians' sojourn there ultimately extended well into the fall.

The synagogue and the meeting house could not be more different stylistically. Kerem Shalom's contemporary sanctuary is all glass, warm natural wood, and geometric space. The modern Ark, the eternal flame, and the *bimah* form the focal point of the room, which is filled with natural light. Plate-glass windows provide stunning views of the surrounding marsh and woodlands. The seating is flexible (and more comfortable than the wooden pews of the meeting house). First Parish moved its baby grand piano to Kerem Shalom for the duration of its stay; the cantor and the host congregation much appreciated the instrument. The room was spacious, yet intimate. The acoustics, warm and crisp. But there was no place to seat the choir.

"Seat the choir." This phrase echoes back more than two centuries to the time of William Emerson, grandfather of Ralph Waldo Emerson. He was called to be minister of First Parish in 1764, a little more than a decade before the beginning of the American Revolution. The battle for independence that began in Concord followed several earlier skirmishes within the parish over music and whether to "seat a choir." In the midst of intensifying political tensions with Britain, the young minister coped with an eighteenth-century version of the "worship wars" within his own parish. In William Emerson's day, young adults met socially with itinerant singing masters like Boston's William Billings and learned how to read music and to sing together in parts. As a young man, William Emerson had participated in these social singing schools. This was the contemporary music that was being introduced into worship. Until then, worship music had been confined to congregational singing of the psalms, led by a deacon who lined out the psalm text, phrase by phrase, to a familiar hymn tune. The congregation would respond after each phrase, echoing the deacon's example. Surviving instructions to singing deacons from this period indicate that the quality of this practice was highly variable, but it was the custom. The idea of a rehearsed choir—and of men and women singing together—was its own kind of worship revolution. Added to that was the introduction of new, freely translated psalms of the classic metrical versions by Tate and Brady, and wholly new hymn texts—considered blasphemy by some—by hymn writers like Isaac Watts.

William Emerson described efforts to adopt contemporary music and worship resources during the eighteenth century in his diaries and letters. He notes, in February 1766, that the congregation "Voted to sing Tate and Bradys version of the Psalms 3 month, Upon Tryal." By June of that year, the congregation had agreed "to sing Dr. Watts psalms and his first book of Hymns in ye Congregation," according to Eleanor Billings in "Music in the Meeting House," *The Meeting House on the Green*. A year later, Emerson noted that a new practice of having the congregation stand to sing made "a few very uneasy."

The congregation continued to wrestle with the adoption of the new way of choral singing as they contemplated physical changes to the meeting house. In May 1774, the Town Meeting "voted to new seat the Meeting House but not to appropriate any part . . . to Singers." Apparently at this point, the new way had not gained enough traction to warrant permanent changes in the meeting house seating. However, six months later, the parish voted "that for ye better and more decent carrying on of public worship, Deacon Wheeler would lead in ye Singing one half of ye Time, and ye Singers the other half, in ye Congregation." Through a process that offers wisdom to succeeding generations, the old way of deacon-led singing and the new way of choral anthems were integrated through a graceful compromise. The choir retained seats among the congregation, presumably rising when it was time to sing together. It would be many years and another renovation before any special accommodation was made for the choir. Yet, a precedent had been set for blending innovation and tradition—eighteenth-century upcycling—in a way that was meaningful to the community.

This systemic precedent served First Parish well during the congregation's six months of exile in 2008. With no space to seat the choir in the synagogue, singers surrounded the congregation, taking seats at the end of each row of chairs and standing in place to sing anthems in surround sound. In this way, the choir members supported congregational singing in this unfamiliar space and smoothly transitioned to anthems by simply rising to their feet. These circumstances also forced the choir to learn a new way of listening to one another and blending their voices. A song leader led the hymns from the *bimah*, along with the other service elements, including the sermon.

The time in the Kerem Shalom sanctuary transformed the role of the choir in worship. In their musical and logistical embrace of the congregation, singers became the walls of First Parish's nomadic tent. The congregation's sojourn in the vineyard of peace became a fruitful time of growth and experimentation rather than just a hardship to endure. Lessons learned in exile enriched the worship experience after the congregation returned to its home on Lexington Road.

Upcycling at First Parish has involved other, subtle physical changes that responded to the needs of a congregation and worship leaders seeking more flexibility. Well before the sanctuary restoration in 2008, the imposing central pulpit was coaxed into a more adaptable role by the discreet installation of retractable wheels. Though this innovation is invisible to the congregation—the pulpit and chancel appear to be wrought of the same piece of wood—the pulpit can be raised onto the wheels and rolled backward. This opens a small but prominent stage area that offers more presentational flexibility. On various occasions, the pulpit has given way to a living nativity, dancers, instrumentalists, singers, and at the winter solstice, a flaming cauldron.

Once the choirs were freed from the confines of the choir loft, it was natural to experiment with more creative ways to use the traditional space. The choir has cast a circle from the four corners of the balcony and sung antiphonal Renaissance motets from the opposing sides. Singers have led congregational rounds while moving in circles around the center of the sanctuary. A drum set now resides near the grand piano downstairs, and a multichannel public address system can be easily set up when that supplement to the sanctuary sound system is required. What looks at first like a rigid liturgical space offers myriad opportunities for upcycling.

What feels contemporary about worship at First Parish is not just the music, because the music is not always contemporary in style. Several innovations in worship design contribute to a contemporary feel in a space that proclaims tradition.

Worship is a team effort. The worship staff (clergy, musician, religious educator, intern) gather for at least one hour every week to evaluate past worship services and to plan for the future. The team's focus is not just on the next Sunday but as far ahead as the next month or sometimes the next year. The members of the team have deep mutual respect and trust for each other, built through working together and keeping lines of communication open. It is a partnership. The service leader of the week establishes the theme but accepts and integrates the voices and visions of colleagues. The team encourages creativity and out-of-the-box thinking. Increasingly, the worship team thinks in terms of a multisensory experience: how to incorporate movement, sight, smell, sound, touch. At an intergenerational Thanksgiving service, the congregation shared a guided meditation that involved mindfully peeling and eating oranges. The scent of those sweet fruits was intoxicating.

Synergy and grace also play a part—unplanned connections often happen during the service. The worship experience can take on a life of its own, exceeding the expectations of careful creators. There is wisdom in allowing for this possibility and trusting it.

Worship engages the head and the heart. The elements of the liturgy encourage both intellectual engagement and spiritual practice. While services vary along the head/heart continuum, there is overall balance. Music of all types (not just multicultural music) is contextualized both by notes in the order of service and through associations revealed within the service. Poetry and story partner with prose and empirical observation. The complexity of Baroque counterpoint is valued as deeply as the simple harmonies of a Taizé chant.

Worship is interactive. The liturgy consistently includes congregational litanies and responsive readings. The new supplement of worship readings from the UUA, *Lifting Our Voices*, has widened the repertoire of readings and broadened the diversity of perspectives. The pulpit and the choir encourage strong congregational singing. They sing songs without the hymnal whenever it is practical. Call and response, rounds, and chants are all part of the repertoire. The organ provides solid support and lifts the congregational singing, but just as often piano, guitar, and other instruments accompany the singing. Every service includes texts and songs that every member knows by heart. Occasionally projected images are used. With the light of the clear windows and scarcity of flat projection surfaces, this is a new frontier in upcycling, but some promising experiments are in progress.

Music leadership is often intergenerational. The children and youth choirs regularly provide anthems and lead the hymn singing, sometimes in partnership with the adult choirs. The congregation sees musicians of all ages as worship leaders, not just performers. Sometimes, the youngest singers have led the congregation to the greatest spiritual depth. Children are always present at the beginning of the service. The message for children is usually linked to the worship theme and provides congregants of all ages with another mode of relating to that theme.

The sanctuary space informs but does not dictate the logistics of worship. Worship leaders have freedom to experiment with the space and sometimes work against the function that the form would suggest. The word is not always central: At this writing, the worship team is planning a service in which the musicians will take over the pulpit area, while the speakers (and the chalice) will be in the choir loft.

The path to innovation at First Parish in Concord has been smoothest when it is paved with respect for tradition; upcycling is best introduced gradually and with opportunities for response and reflection. Yet, it is not halted by resistance. Upcycling efforts are usually proposed in a spirit of experimentation. Moving the choirs from the rear loft to the floor was not initially popular with all choir members—or all congregants. But when presented and attempted with a "let's see what happens" attitude, congregants gradually adjusted their expectations and accepted the change. These days, the choirs usually sing from the front of the sanctuary or in the aisles, or in some other formation yet to be devised by the choir director. On Sundays when the choir returns to the loft to sing the anthems and support the hymns, it is not surprising to hear "it was so lovely to hear the voices wafting down from the choir loft again," and "I missed seeing the choir's faces up front" in two successive conversations. Evidence of similar disagreements on the path to the new way/old way compromise achieved during William Emerson's ministry reminds us that controversy has always existed in religious communities. When we seek to modernize today, we act in some solidarity with our predecessors, and this is a comfort.

Upcycling Our Hymn Singing

DONALD MILTON III

When I was hired by Dixboro United Methodist Church, just outside of Ann Arbor, Michigan, to work with their praise and worship band called Joyful Noise, I was just twenty-one years old. Every Tuesday night, I worked with their pianist, drummer, guitar players, and singers, and helped them arrange the music for their contemporary service on Sunday morning. It was a great part-time job for a college student; the people were wonderful, the work was fun. But I couldn't stand the music. This was a few years before I became a Unitarian Universalist; I was, at the time, an ardent and moderately intolerant atheist. Beyond the overtly Christian message that I then found unpalatable, the music itself, with its repetitive choruses and saccharin melodies, lacked depth, beauty, and something to latch onto. But there I was every Tuesday night listening to Joyful Noise play "Our God Is an Awesome God," and "These Are the Days of Elijah."

Working with this praise band did nothing to improve my negative preconceived notions about praise music, which remained for me a caricature. You might see the same picture in your mind's eye: a rock band playing slow repetitive choruses, huge throngs of people staring at a screen, arms raised in the air, singing "God Music."

Fast forward almost a decade, and I was attending the Unitarian Universalist Musicians Network (UUMN) conference in Tulsa,

Oklahoma. This was many years after my experience with Joyful Noise and several years into my tenure as the music director at the UU Congregation of Atlanta, where I had learned to celebrate different worship practices from a multitude of faith traditions.

All Souls Unitarian Church in Tulsa had gone through a major transformation. During the summer, when it holds only one service, it had offered the sanctuary to New Dimensions, a church of predominantly African-American Pentecostal Universalist Christians. Many members of All Souls chose to attend the New Dimensions services at 11:30 and revel in the high-energy praise music that was a centerpiece of their worship. At the end of that summer, New Dimensions decided to disband its church and join the All Souls community. This was a seismic shift for everyone involved and included the hiring of New Dimensions music director David Smith to help combine the New Dimensions spirit energy with the mostly Euro-American, intellectually focused UU service.

The All Souls story was well known in UU circles as we gathered in Tulsa for our UUMN conference. This is many years after my experience with Joyful Noise and several years into my tenure as the music director at the UU Congregation of Atlanta where I had learned to celebrate different worship practices in the multitude of faith tradition. Though I may have been more accepting by that time, I still harbored a deep dislike of praise music. On the Friday night of the conference, the New Dimensions band was going to hold a full praise and worship service. I had planned to skip it, but it was pouring rain and I didn't have anywhere else to be, so I reluctantly entered the sanctuary.

I was a little on edge; if they were going to break into "Our God Is an Awesome God" in a UU congregation, I would surely be uncomfortable. My fears were very quickly put to rest.

The service opened with "Enter, Rejoice, and Come In" from the UU hymnal, *Singing the Living Tradition*, but unlike I had ever heard it. The drums were swinging, the bass was running, and the piano was flying all over the place. The song was familiar (though I was not particularly fond of it) and upcycled into something that changed the feel and more accurately conveyed the message. The first song invited me in and convinced me that "today will be a joyful day." The band seamlessly transitioned into new arrangements of familiar hymns like "Come, Come, Whoever You Are" and "This Little Light of Mine." It peppered the set by incorporating songs like "Love Lift Us Up Where We Belong" and "Let It Be." It used choruses from praise and worship songs but put them into a UU context and paired them with songs inside UU tradition. It took us on a musical journey that was soul stirring, healing, uplifting, and musically excellent.

I had a change of heart that night. I saw that there were benefits to praise-style music: The simple, repetitive choruses are easy to sing, which invites people to use their whole voices. The transitions between songs are full of joyful surprises. Along with the incredible band, you find yourself singing in a endorphin-fueled euphoria, far from the ultra-intellectual space typical of UU services. It was similar to the feeling I get onstage at a concert. How could I bring some of these feelings into my congregation?

Why Upcyle?

When addressing the UUMN at our 2008 annual conference, former president of the UUA Bill Sinkford said, "For many years musicians have been carrying the spiritual water for Unitarian Universalists." He elaborated that, in a religion so consistently focused on the head, music opens our hearts to something outside ourselves. Music sets the tone of the service so we can receive the message in the most impactful way.

The most common way we access music on a Sunday morning is through our shared UU hymnody. As Unitarian Universalists, we draw from many sources and do not share a common lectionary. On any given Sunday, congregations may have vastly different worship topics. But our hymnals are something that UUs in Atlanta have in common with UUs in Albuquerque. The content of our hymnal doesn't always touch on the many sources we have to cover. In trying to be pluralistic, we have a lot of vague texts, and while our hymnals are full of beautiful melodies, many were written in the eighteenth and nineteenth centuries. Like many spiritual texts, they have archaic material that is powerful and useful and that needs to be put into a new context to have an effect on our congregation.

Upcycling is a way to make some of hymns feel relevant again. It's a way to inject some spirit energy into services and stop feeling as if we're going through the motions or, even worse, that the hymn singing is just filler between the wordy parts. Our hymnals provide incredible source material for this journey.

Often, singing a hymn exactly as written in the hymnal, with organ or piano accompaniment, is just what the service needs. It is part of our cultural heritage as Unitarian Universalists and can definitely enhance the message, vibe, and flow of a service. It also serves the people in our congregation who are looking for the familiarity of traditional worship. Yet, if this is the only way your congregation accesses the music, or if this type of musical experience doesn't serve your more contemporary messages, you may want to upcycle the hymns. And you might be surprised to find what you can do.

Breaking the Mold

There are innumerable ways to upcycle our hymns. Before my experience in Tulsa, I had put my own spin on our hymnals: adding a drum here and there, doing some hymns on guitar, occasionally incorporating nonhymnal songs by either rote teaching or projecting lyrics. My experience at the UUMN conference inspired me to break the mold. Hymns can give us a deep well of creative water to draw from; there is a wide spectrum of things we can do to enhance our hymn singing. Music directors throughout our movement are finding ways to upcycle hymns every week.

There are three levels of hymn upcycling. *Dusting off* is to change simple things to make the hymns more beautiful and to freshen up congregational singing. *New paint* is to make bigger changes that help us experience the hymns differently, delving deeper into the meaning or even changing the meaning by how we approach them. The third level, *full remodel*, keeps the bones but comes at the music in a whole different way to create an experience far different from traditional hymn singing.

Three hymns serve as examples for all three levels: "Come Thou Fount of Every Blessing" with words written in 1758 and set to music in 1813; "Spirit of Life," which is considered the UU "Amazing Grace" and sung every Sunday in many congregations; and "Meditation on Breathing," a more contemporary favorite written as a response to the September 11 attacks.

Many songs in our UU hymnals have already been upcycled. We've altered pronouns to make them more inclusive. We've taken new poems and set them to melodies that are hundreds of years old. We've softened some patriarchal and theistic language to make some hymns more welcoming. I have occasionally *downcycled* some of the hymns in *Singing the Living Tradition* to be more true to their original religious traditions. The hymnal is a great starting point when planning a musical experience.

Dusting Off Old Favorites

As worship planners, sometimes we feel as though we've fallen into a hymn-singing rut. Every congregation has its favorite hymns, and over time, singing them can go past the warmth of familiarity and feel stale or dusty. Sometimes we need to get out of our old habits to experience the music with the same joy and meaning as the first time we sang it. Organists have been doing this for centuries with reharmonizations and a key change before the last verse, but we can make other small changes to perk up our ears and instill a breath of fresh air. Adding hand drums or shakers to upbeat songs is a great way to infuse energy. Alternately, we sing many hymns in our hymnals, particularly hymns with multiple verses, as fast as we can just to get through them, when slowing them down can reveal subdivisions that give the pieces new life. Start by grabbing a metronome (or downloading one on your phone), and checking the tempo marking in the hymnal. You'll see how we sing many hymns much faster than the composers intended.

"Come Thou Fount of Every Blessing": A slight change in instrumentation can give a favorite song a sonic facelift. Songs with soaring, beautiful melodies like "Come Thou Fount" can gain a lot by simply adding a melody instrument like a flute, oboe, violin, or cello to the piano or organ accompaniment. This technique also gives the congregation members another sound to sing along with, which can encourage them to free their voices.

"Meditation on Breathing": Even this newer hymn can feel old if it's accompanied on the piano. This song, along with many others by composers like Jim Scott and Shelley Jackson Denham, feel more natural on guitar, which can really change how the congregation experiences the songs. The composer of "Meditation on Breathing," Sarah Dan Jones, often leads the song with just a drum.

"Spirit of Life": A simple way to dust off an old favorite like this one is to adjust the tempo. If we feel that a meditative song like "Spirit of Life" or "What Wondrous Love Is This" is plodding, taking it a few clicks faster can make it feel as though it's rolling forward and more hopeful. We can also take it a few clicks slower or drop the piano part and sing it a cappella so that people can really focus on the words and harmonies.

Many congregations consider "Spirit of Life" an untouchable hymn, thinking that any changes made would not be worth the outrage they would provoke. In my congregation, one untouchable hymn is "We Would Be One," a pillar for our members, especially our elders, and one of the most requested songs for memorial services and even weddings. Swinging this song, and adding some percussion and maybe a saxophone, would be fun but wouldn't be worth the complaints I would receive after the service. I could judiciously dust off "We Would Be One" if I had a string quartet, a brass quintet, or other classical instrumentalists. Adding them to the hymn in the existing arrangement would enrich the sound and the texture without changing the grand feel.

A New Coat of Paint

If you've had success with simple changes, you might try to go further. A fresh coat of paint can really liven up a familiar room, making it feel new again. An important factor as you start to make bigger changes is quality. We all have congregants who are going to be against any changes you make. If we put a band together or try to jazz up a hymn and it falls apart, their fears will be realized. The new experience must be positive, allowing your program to build momentum.

Major changes in how a song is orchestrated could incorporate many instruments and change the entire sound palette. They could alter the musical style from classical to jazz, folk, or rock. Or strip down a song and just repeat the chorus in a slow and meditative way.

My senior minister's favorite hymn is "Woyaya" in *Singing the Journey*. If left to his own devices, we might sing it every week. The congregation is very familiar with it and enjoys singing it, but one Sunday, the jolly, frolicking, hopeful accompaniment didn't fit the message, but the text, "It will be hard we know, and the road will be muddy and rough," definitely did. So I used a hand drum, and we sang it really slowly. Feet-stuck-in-the-mud slow. It changed from being a hopeful song about journeying together into a visceral song about hard work and struggle. It was the same song but an entirely different worship element.

"Come Thou Fount of Every Blessing": My favorite way to alter this song is by changing the meter, adding or taking away a beat from each measure. I change it from 3/2 (six quarter notes in a measure) to 5/4 (five quarter notes in a measure). By removing a beat from each measure, you propel the song forward, adding energy and excitement. The melody remains the same, and the rhythmic changes are intuitive and easy to pick up. This new feel lends itself to adding percussion or a whole band.

"Spirit of Life": Since we usually use this song during meditative times, I occasionally slow it down and have the choir sing the harmony, so the whole congregation lives inside the sound. We also usually pair it with the Spanish lyrics. Our congregation has very few Spanish speakers, but adding a foreign language to our most beloved hymn is an expression of our values and our yearning to live in an inclusive society. One congregation member has rearranged the chords and does a happy, bouncy version for our children's chapel, but I still file it under untouchable and don't use it in "main stage" worship.

"Meditation on Breathing": This song is so appealing in its simplicity. The same simplicity opens the song up to be arranged or reharmonized and enjoyed in many genres. We've done this piece jazzy, folksy, with a Latin feel, and with an earth-centered feel. With versatile musicians, changing genres spices up hymns that feel stale, including Christmas carols.

A Full Remodel

Several years ago I put together a music Sunday service titled, "I Hate Praise Music." The evocative title filled the pews, and the service began with ten minutes of UU hymns upcycled into praise and worship splendor. The band rocked its way through a medley of "I Know This Rose Will Open," "Come, Come, Whoever You Are," "Gathered Here," "You've Got to Do When the Spirit Says Do," and James Taylor's "How Sweet It Is to Be Loved by You." People were definitely shocked, most in a good way, and the vibe in the room was electric.

The service included several more medleys and mash-ups. Many people were enamored with the music and wanted it every Sunday. Others were merely polite after the service. We now do all of our hymns in praise style once a month.

Putting together good medleys and mash-ups is a lot like remodeling a kitchen: it's time consuming, expensive, and worth it. You will need to compensate your music director for the hours it takes to arrange and rehearse the fully remodeled hymns.

Nearly every song in every medley or mash-up has already been upcycled with a thick coat of paint. The goal in hymn singing is always to connect to the message of the service. A well-crafted medley can make the truth stickier and help the congregants go deeper. The logic-minded people in the pews will delight in the connections between the hymns and the sermon.

Medleys and mash-ups have different compositions but a similar goal: momentum! Every time you change a song or change a key, the energy in the room leaps up. Even in medleys that are slow and contemplative, the elation in the changes helps drive home the point. It's similar to that feeling you get when your favorite song comes on the radio. You're flooded with memories and emotions that are amplified by the sudden surprise.

In medleys, you need to consider the arc. Is there a story arc or an emotional arc? Where are you headed? Do you want to return to the beginning? I like to start medleys with "There Is More Love Somewhere," because the text tells you you're looking for something and the medley won't be over until you find it. From there, you can move into UU hymns, like "Standing on the Side of Love" or "Love Will Guide Us." You can break the mold and incorporate non-UU songs into your medley, like "One Love, One Heart" or "All You Need Is Love." For the final verse, I go up a key or two and return to the first song with new lyrics: "There is more love right here. I'm gonna keep on 'cause I found it." We've hit the story arc and the emotional arc, a clear beginning and a clear end.

Mash-ups involve a touch of serendipity. Finding two melodies of the same length (or divisible) with similar chord structure so one can be sung over the other's music without clashing is a difficult task. Often I feel as though I stumble upon a mash-up when I'm working on medleys. For instance, while practicing music for our Thanksgiving service, I realized that "Come and Go With Me" mashes up beautifully with "Oh We Give Thanks." I was elated. We sang "Oh We Give Thanks" alone, two verses of "Come and Go With Me," and then sang both songs over the "Oh We Give Thanks" chords. When I realized we could sing the South African freedom song "Oh, Freedom" over George Michael's "Freedom 90," I smiled for a week.

In both mash-ups and medleys, transitions are incredibly important. First, they need to be well planned. Are you staying in the same key? If not, how are you going to pivot? Will the whole band play the pivot or just the pianist? Are you changing tempo? If not, who will lead the change, the pianist or the drummer? A little bit of Hollywood magic is necessary to keep people engaged mentally and musically in the transitions. They want to feel the momentum swell but not hear you tip your hand. To make it work, the transitions have to be smooth, and that takes a lot of practice.

"Come Thou Fount of Every Blessing": I like to start with the rocking 5/4 version described in the "New Paint" section. There are two hymns in *Singing the Journey* in the same 5/4 meter as our upcycled "Come Thou Fount": "The Fire of Commitment" and "Turn the World Around." Looking closer, all three can be sung comfortably in D major and have the same tempo, making them prime medley material. The texts have excellent transition points: "Come Thou Fount . . ." "We come from the fire . . ." "When the fire of commitment . . ." I would lay it out like this:

"Come Thou Fount"	verse 1
"Turn the World Around"	verse 1
"Come Thou Fount"	verse 2
"The Fire of Commitment"	chorus
"Come Thou Fount"	verse 3

"Meditation on Breathing": This piece fits beautifully into slow medleys, but I love to use it in mash-ups. Because the melody is easy to reharmonize, singing it over a lot of different chords still sounds great. It already has a descant melody, and the whole song is only eight measures, so it can fit with other eight bar choruses, you can double it over a sixteen-bar chorus, or even sing it four times over a thirty-two-bar verse and chorus.

When I was the music director for the Service of the Living Tradition at the UUA General Assembly in 2015, the Supreme Court was preparing to hear the case on marriage equality, so I put together a mash-up of "Same Love," "Waiting on the World to Change," and "People Get Ready," followed by "Meditation on Breathing." All the songs have very similar chords and can be sung over the same repeating pattern. Throughout the song, we returned to "Meditation on Breathing," eventually combining it with "People Get Ready" and "Same Love" individually. At the end of the arrangement, we sang all of the melodies at the same time.

The Future of Music Is Collaboration and Connection

Let's look at two possible openings for a Sunday morning service. The music director stands up and says, "Good morning. Our first hymn is going to be number 123 in your gray hymnal, 'Spirit of Life.' Again, that's number 123, 'Spirit of Life.' Please rise in body or in spirit." There is a pregnant pause as everyone fumbles through their hymnals, while standing. A four-measure introduction is played, the congregation sings the melody of "Spirit of Life" with the piano accompaniment, and then everyone sits down.

The minister walks to the pulpit and says, "Good morning, we are called to worship by the words of Unitarian Universalist minister Peter Raible . . ." They read the words, the minister sits, and we move on the next separate piece of music or liturgy.

Imagine a very different opening. The lights are lowered. A soloist walks up to a microphone and sings "Spirit of Life" a capella. As the soloist finishes, the pianist takes over playing the chord structure of "Spirit of Life" but not the melody. The minister or liturgist stands up and slowly walks up to a different microphone. As the piano continues playing, she recites words from Deuteronomy, adapted by Peter Raible:

> We build on a foundation we did not lay.
> We warm ourselves at fires we did not light.
> We sit in the shade of trees we did not plant.
> We drink from wells we did not dig.

We profit from persons we did not know.
We are ever bound in community.

Next, the lyrics to "Spirit of Life" are projected on to the screen
(or printed with permission in the order of service), and the soloist
gestures to the congregation. Everyone knows to sing along from
the nonverbal cues. The congregation and soloist sing together
with the piano. When they finish, the piano continues as the minister says these words by Anthony Makar:

As Unitarian Universalists we believe:
Truth is larger than any one book or way;
Religion and science go hand-in-hand;
Integrity requires freedom of conscience;
Diversity is something to celebrate;
In the struggle for justice, we come alive.
Our highest aspiration and calling is Love.
(*piano stops*)
Whoever you are, whatever path you are on, you are
    welcome here!

We experience a few moments of silence; then the soloist
gestures to the congregation and the choir members (who have
already rehearsed this), and they sing "Spirit of Life" a third time,
a little bit slower, a cappella, in harmony.

The congregation takes a second to breathe. They have just
experienced the opening hymn and the call to worship in a deeper,
far more impactful way. We've used an upcycled hymn to blend
together two worship elements that would have been fine on their
own but together have a powerful, memorable effect on each other,
the whole far greater than the sum of its parts.

We sing a couple of rousing versions of "We're Gonna Sit at
the Welcome Table" with piano, guitar, drums, tambourine, and so
on. Then a reading from an undocumented immigrant waiting to
be deported. We return to "We're Gonna Sit at the Welcome Table"

but sing it slowly, out of meter, with no accompaniment. This song of welcome has turned into a song of yearning for acceptance. We could stop there or find another reading that brings us back to joy and acceptance. We could sing the first verse again, starting slow with sparse accompaniment, but accelerating, with crescendos. We repeat the first verse until it's loud and raucous; we again believe that all people belong at the welcome table.

* * *

Almost every movie, television show, and online video is now an incredible combination of words, images, and music. We can learn a lot from those creating this meaningful content and start incorporating images and videos into our services. We can weave music throughout our service elements. In the future, music directors and ministers will work together to craft worship services that break the Protestant mold and are less "plug and play" and more collaborative. The services will have more short elements, more multimedia, more room for silence and reflection, fewer seams, and greater impact.

These changes need a worship team that works closely together. There will be a lot of trial and error and a lot of rehearsal time. The result could be impactful worship services that change people's lives, that they can't stop thinking about, and can't wait until the next Sunday to experience again. Worship services brimming with the "spiritual water of Unitarian Universalism."

Coffee Hour Central

SETH FISHER

The story begins in a familiar way—a very large and aging church building with a very small and aging church membership. When I took my post as congregational development minister, I was given the task of bringing in more people who would consequently contribute more money, with the understanding that that's what we needed to save the church. And this seemed obvious, because it was certainly not going to be able to sustain itself at its current membership or funding levels. We made some changes to Sunday morning worship right away and put a little more effort into the planning of those services with the goal of creating the best worship experience we could. I also began to stand outside in front of the church before the service on Sunday mornings to welcome people and greet anyone passing by. I personally said hello to newcomers and tried to make them feel welcome. I encouraged members to invite friends to church. I was doing everything I could think of to get more people to come to Sunday morning worship and trying as hard as I could to get them to return once they did. But it soon occurred to me that if only a quarter of the people who visited our church came back, we would be growing; maybe they weren't coming back or weren't coming in the first place because we didn't have what they were looking for. So I took a break from thinking about trying to be more inviting, and I started to think more about what we were inviting them to.

This meant thinking about what we were there to do in the first place. We needed to think about our mission, about what church was and what church was for. My working definition of church is a place where we can become better people and build a better world together. This seems like something that people would almost universally appreciate. Who wouldn't want to be part of that? But I've often talked with people about Unitarian Universalism in a conversation that goes something like this:

People tell me that they don't have any interest in church, and I say, "Our church is different. We don't have a single doctrine. We think that there is some truth in all of the world's faiths and philosophies and that people should be allowed to figure out for themselves what makes sense to them."

They say something like, "Well, that's what I think too."

And I say, "We believe that everyone has inherent value and that we're all connected. We should accept one another and encourage each other to grow."

They say, "I totally agree!"

I say, "We come together as a community to support one another and live out our shared values."

And they say, "That sounds awesome! Where do I sign up?!"

Then I say, "Great! Come to our big old building on Sunday morning to sing hymns and listen to a sermon."

And they say, "Huh?" The look of excitement vanishes, immediately replaced with a look of disappointment because they had just become convinced that they had found something new and transformative to fill a very real need in their life, only to find that I was just talking about church after all.

We need to take a step back and distinguish between "church" and *church*. "Church" is candles and piano music and vestments and readings. *Church* is a community where people grow together and help each other create lives of meaning. "Church" is great if you're into that sort of thing. It's always been part of what we do, and it always will be, because it works for a lot of people. But *church* is what we're really here for. "Church" is one way of doing *church*, but if it's the only way, then we're going to fail to reach a lot of people who don't have any interest in "church" but are really longing for *church* and may not even know it. We're not in the business of getting people to sing hymns and listen to sermons. We're in the business of transforming lives. And this is something that's in demand. Many people want more meaning in their lives, want to make a difference in the world, and want to be part of a community that supports these endeavors. People genuinely desire this kind of community, but many don't see any connection between this and a traditional Sunday morning church service. So why are we trying to squeeze everyone into that model? When we realize that what we traditionally think of as "church" is only one way to carry out our mission, we can open our eyes to the opportunities we have to invite people into our community in new ways. Instead of trying to get more people to come to "church," as in Sunday morning services, we can think about how to get more people to come to *church*, as in becoming part of a transformational community.

Once we were able to look at our church as a place for transformation, we started to look at what we had to offer beyond the Sunday service. The church had an enormous auditorium that was never filled for services, but musicians loved to play in it because of the excellent acoustics. We had an art gallery upstairs, and a dozen resident artists with studios throughout the building. We had a lunch program that served food to hungry people in our neighborhood six days a week. We also had other connections with the community that weren't always apparent to people who visited on Sunday mornings. For example, we were part of an interfaith group that held informal discussions over lunch once a month, and had a theater space that frequently hosted works with a social justice angle. Doing this spiritual audit allowed us to see that we had much more to offer than was obvious at first glance. We had a veritable buffet of different ways to feed the soul, and this was what we needed to invite people to.

So once we realized that we had all these assets, our invitation took a very different shape. We wanted to let people know about everything we had to offer without making them sit through a Sunday service, if that was going to be an obstacle for them. We started inviting people directly to the coffee hour after the Sunday service and made that hour a sort of open house and showcase of everything that was going on at church. We put art from the gallery on rotating display in the lobby. We invited musicians from the community to use the stage for an open jam or to promote their projects. Volunteers were able to simply show up and help out with serving lunch. We informed people about the various programs going on in the church at other times—an interfaith meditation group, a creative writing group, and so on. We also told them about events connected with the larger community around us, like a clean-up day at a nearby park, a social justice march, a street fair, and more. The idea was to create a sort of social gateway for personal growth and community connection of all kinds where people could find whatever we had to offer that might feed their soul.

And it worked! Slowly but surely, people who wouldn't normally be interested in a Sunday morning church service began to come check us out. Some even stuck around. Ironically, a few decided to come early the following week to check out the worship service. The regulars tended to stay longer, too. More people came during the coffee hour than for the service, which helped us all build community together. The coffee hour became a social event for both members and newcomers where people could meet, experience community, and learn about all that we were doing in a way that was welcoming and specific to their needs. What we ended up with didn't look a whole lot different from our usual coffee hour. It was just a new and improved version—a little more vibrant, a little more welcoming, a little more deliberately connected with our larger mission, and consequently a little more like the Beloved Community that we strive for.

But it wasn't magic, and it wasn't perfect. I definitely learned a few things the hard way as I went along. First, it takes a team and the whole community to get on board. With a really small congregation, I thought I could just meet and greet all the newcomers myself, but that turned out not to be true. We needed a team of people who really understood the whole idea of welcoming others into the community in whatever way would speak to them. These aren't the same brief conversations a good greeter might have with a newcomer. They require people who can go deep quickly and not only make others feel welcome but also help direct them toward whatever resources will help feed their soul. These people need to be something like a cross between a cocktail party host and a spiritual guide—someone who can really listen and make the connection between a person who wants to give back and an opportunity to volunteer in a meal program, or between a person who is looking for personal growth and a weekly meditation group, a person who needs connection and a small group ministry, and so on. It's important to have as many of the ministries and opportunities as possible present so that people can find what speaks to them, but they will still need some help and guidance from a warm and knowledgeable guide; this isn't a role that one person can take on alone.

There also needs to be a general welcome from the entire community, not just a small core of trained members. Early on in this experiment, someone showed up for coffee hour before the worship service had let out. As the visitor started to pour a cup of coffee, a longtime member told this visitor that coffee was for after the service and that they needed to wait. Not very welcoming! So it's important to have a small group of people who are good, welcoming listeners and are well informed about all of the opportunities in the community. It's also important to make sure that the whole church community knows that you are deliberately inviting people directly to the coffee hour. They are welcome guests.

We also created a Facebook page and a meet-up group to brand the coffee hour as its own weekly event and invited people to come and experience all we had to offer. This helped create the understanding that the coffee hour was an opportunity to invite people into our community and that it was more than an addition to the worship service. This little bit of marketing was valuable on its own, but it took more than that. You can invite people to an event with a little of everything, where they will find a community interested in helping them connect with whatever they need to feed their soul, but only a brave few will probably accept that invitation. We had a lot more success in getting new people through the door when we invited musicians to an open jam, artists to see a new exhibit, and volunteers to help feed people. Once they showed up, they could learn about everything else that was going on, but the idea of a one-stop shop for spiritual growth was just too general and too daunting for many. People need to have a much clearer and specific idea of what they are getting into before they take that first bold step into a building with strangers. They are much more likely to come when they know that there is something there that will speak to them.

You can probably do this in your community as well. The essential elements are a team clear on the overall concept and committed to supporting it; a spiritual audit of what the church has to offer people who are looking for community, connection, and greater meaning in their lives; an event at which to display those opportunities; and folks who help newcomers find their unique way to connect.

Your congregation will be an embodiment of your particular community, but some version of this effort could transfer to almost any congregation. What's even more transferrable and ultimately more important is the process of getting in touch with your mission and asking yourself where your church's assets meet the needs of those looking for a community. What obstacles might you inadvertently be putting in their way? What resources can you provide for people who want to have a fuller, more meaningful life? How can you invite them to be part of your community and connect with those resources? Think bigger or, rather, deeper about your mission and your offering. Because, as fewer people seem to be interested in "church," their need for life-giving, transformative community is more relevant than ever. We have all that, and a cup of coffee.

Join Our Cause, Not Our Club

CAREY McDONALD AND SARAH GIBB MILLSPAUGH

As the movement for Black lives and liberation grew in 2016, First Parish in Malden, Massachusetts, like so many other congregations, knew that it had to act. Carey, a member of this congregation (and co-author of this essay) remembers:

> After reading *The New Jim Crow* by Michelle Alexander as a congregation, we voted to put up a banner showing our support for Black Lives Matter. We also knew a banner isn't enough; it's just a ticket to the conversation. As a next step, we offered a public forum on what it means to support the movement for Black lives in our community, cosponsored with another UU congregation just down the road. Fifty people showed up on a Saturday afternoon to hear organizers and activists from the local Black Lives Matter chapter and allied organizations like the NAACP and Asian Pacific Islanders for Black Lives talk about their work. We received a great write-up in the local weekly paper, carrying the message to hundreds, if not thousands, more.
>
> The following Sunday, which was the first weekend after the presidential election, we received more visitors than I've ever seen at our small church. People were looking for a place that shared their values and their sense of

urgency in a time of frustration and pain. They knew they could find that in our congregation, in part because we had taken these public actions to show our faithful commitments to justice and compassion. We had to show up before anyone else would.

We must show up—in our values, principles, actions, and ministry—before a wider community will want show up to be part of that ministry. As Unitarian Universalists, we have often approached our congregational life by focusing our resources and services on existing, highly committed members. But this fundamental truth, that people must experience our faith commitments from the very beginning, anchors the outreach required for our faith communities to live into the calling of our times.

Chances are, you didn't grow up Unitarian Universalist. Even if you did, you made a conscious choice to stay Unitarian Universalist or to return again to the faith. Each of us constantly makes choices about our religious participation, our identity, the faith we claim as ours. So what brought you here? What kept you here? What brings you back, again and again? These days, your choice to belong to a UU community is a faithful adventure through shifting perspectives, and a movement toward new possibilities for our congregations and ourselves. How, then, do we help people make those choices and build those commitments, particularly for the first time?

It begins with empathy, the ability to put on someone else's shoes and experience Unitarian Universalism with their heart and mind. We cultivate empathy all the time in our congregations: in worship, programs, activities, and service projects. We cultivate empathy for those people who mainstream society leaves on the margins, both inside and outside our congregations—immigrant children running for their lives, victims of police brutality, single parents living in poverty, and so on.

If we are to live up to our faith's calling and embrace those at the margins, we need to reimagine, redesign, and repurpose the way we "do church." We must upcycle our faith communities by cultivating the same kind of empathy for a new kind of person: those people who have not found us yet and who would find profound meaning in what we have to offer.

The Changing Religious Landscape

Attitudes toward religion are changing in America. The trends tell us that many people who share values, hopes, and dreams with Unitarian Universalists are reluctant to identify with organized religion—either because they've been hurt by it, found it hollow, or never experienced it in the first place. The number of people who don't identify with any religion in particular—dubbed *nones* in a Pew Forum on Religion and Life study—has steeply risen in the past twenty years. The nones comprise every age group, every racial/ethnic category, and every region of the United States. Young adults have led this trend; according to the Pew Forum, between 2007 and 2014, the percentage of people in the Millennial generation (b. 1981–1996) who are nonreligious jumped from 25 percent to 34 percent, now the single most common religious identification for this generation. But, between 2007 and 2014, the number of nonreligious baby boomers (b. 1946–1964) also grew from 14 percent to 17 percent, and nonreligious Generation X (b. 1965–1980) grew from 19 percent to 23 percent. The trend away from religion holds true for adults of all ages, as every other generational cohort has seen the number of religiously unaffiliated people increase.

While atheism and agnosticism are on the rise, the vast majority of nones believe in a higher power, and many nones have an active spiritual life. The Pew Forum survey found that nones as a group are more likely to pray daily than many religiously identified people. Research by Professor of Religious Studies Elizabeth Drescher shows that nones' spirituality is often eclectic, drawing from more than one source for wisdom and inspiration, and is often functional, basing itself in "what works" rather than in a single tradition's grand narrative (for example, enjoying Catholic Mass for the peaceful feeling it gives on Christmas Eve, and yoga with chanting for the peaceful feeling it gives each week in class).

Many Unitarian Universalists hope that these trends will drive people toward our faith movement, with our historic embrace of humanism on the one hand and practical religion and ritual on the other. We are indeed a wonderful place for people with eclectic, functional beliefs, for atheists and agnostics and believers in God. But hope is not enough; we must also reorient our ministries to make them meaningful and accessible to spiritual seekers at every stage in their faith journey, and begin to build those relationships long before the threshold of traditional membership in a congregation.

When Tera Klein arrived at Throop Unitarian Universalist Church in Pasadena, California, as its newly settled minister, she found a congregation already committed to environmental sustainability. "We realized," she says, "that Earth Day was actually a high holy day for us." Weaving together the environmental, activist, and theological strains of the congregation, Throop quickly became known as a force for ecological change in the community, or sometimes, more simply, as "the church with the garden." The garden became a symbol for the beating heart of the church and a way to get the members *out* and bring the community *in*. In the weeks preceding what is now called eARTh Day at Throop, the congregation spiritually prepares itself to rededicate its energies to the interconnected web of life. The congregation has welcomed many new members who got their start in the garden. By integrating its ecological mission at all levels, and opening up that ministry to people at every stage of commitment, Throop has found new energy and greater impact in its ministry.

What would make someone want to walk through our doors for the first time? Not just a general feeling of community with strangers. What *attracts* people to a congregation or religious community and what *keeps* them are different things. People are attracted by the opportunity for meaning making. They remain as members because of the community and friendships they build.

People don't come because they are searching for friends or a community per se; they are looking for spiritual deepening for themselves and their family and only then find a community that enriches the meaning-based experience and makes them want to return.

In his book *American Grace*, sociologist Robert Putnam identifies some key trends in American religious practice. He writes: "Americans may select their congregations primarily because of theology and worship, but the social investment made within that congregation appears to be what keeps them there." This dynamic is at play within Unitarian Universalism, most recently in the 2014 Multicultural Ministries Sharing Project. This survey of Unitarian Universalists from marginalized groups (related to gender identity, sexual orientation, race/ethnicity, ability, and more) asked respondents why they first decided to attend their congregation and why they continued to attend. The number-one response for the decision to attend was "I wanted to deepen my spiritual life," and the number-one response for staying was "I love the community of people."

For lesbian, gay, bisexual, transgender, and queer (LGBTQ) people, just as for all people, community acceptance certainly matters. But alone, it's not enough, because there are so many other LGBTQ-welcoming faith communities. Unitarian Universalism has been a pioneering American denomination in accepting the full spectrum of gender and sexuality, and we can be thankful that so many others now share our values! While a sense of community may keep people coming back, it's the spiritual deepening, the ways they hope to enhance their experience of thinking, feeling, and being in the world, that draws them in.

The trends show that fewer and fewer people are coming to our congregations because they are motivated to "join a club." In our increasingly interconnected, socially networked communities, people can easily find a social club: the Left-Handed Knitters Circle, the Vegan Brunch Meet-up, the Wednesday Night Ultimate Frisbee League, and the LGBTQ Family Supper Club all offer camaraderie and the opportunity to build friendships with like-minded people. Further, with each successive generation, American culture is making us less and less institutionalist, meaning that Millennials and what's currently dubbed the iGeneration (b. after 1996) are even less likely than Generation X and baby boomers to seek out long-term institutional affiliations. We see this in everything from involvement in traditional civic organizations (e.g., the Rotary Club) to voting patterns and reported trust in institutions (both public and private).

That distance from institutions, however, stands in contrast to younger Americans' hunger to engage with the causes that those institutions supposedly exist to serve. A cause is an expression of something we identify with on a core level. A cause is action oriented, working to create change within us and beyond us. "Spiritual deepening" is a cause. So is "being a good parent" or "living a meaningful life." A cause is "really feeling my connection with all life" or "opening up my heart to experience those I fear as my neighbors, too." Justice issues are also causes, including their deeply rooted meaning making and spiritual aspects that are more important than ever. The dedication to the cause leads younger generations away from traditional institutions, because they see those institutions as unable or unwilling to truly advance those causes. Can our institutional structures evolve to serve their original purpose?

How do we connect with the hundreds, perhaps thousands, of others who live near us who would thrive in Unitarian Universalism? Partly by what we say, partly by how we say it, and partly by what we offer. And for both what we offer and what we communicate about it, we need to understand what a person feels. What does it take to translate, adapt, or upcycle what we offer to ensure that we connect with that person? We need to shift our perspective from how we get people through our doors, which might have been our original goal, to how we are creating a valuable experience for all people.

What You Say

Upcycle your congregation's message to strip away the institution and focus on the action. When you describe what your congregation offers, think in terms of "joining our cause" instead of "joining our club." Show what your congregation does and how it helps people live better lives and make a better world.

The Unitarian Universalist Church of Berkeley has a knack for going where the action is. Its members have been attending the San Francisco Gay Pride parade for years, but recently they added a Martin Luther King Day march in El Cerrito, the Berkeley Solano Stroll, and post-election vigils in Oakland to their travel schedule. Always recognizable in their bright, gold-colored "Standing on the Side of Love" T-shirts, they have also created brochures and handouts that describe their congregation's social justice ministry and activism (recycled from one event to another). "When I was walking home from the Hands Around Lake Merritt event, a couple people stopped me because they recognized the shirts," says longtime lay leader Linda Laskowski. "They each said something about their experience with the church or the music. It really helps the visibility to use those gold shirts." The church has extended that gold to a bright new website and an active social media presence. With an outreach team in place within the congregation, the members have increased their reach and visibility in their area by showing up and being consistent in their messaging.

You can start thinking like Berkeley by taking a second look at what you show to the world on your website and in your brochures. When the UUA recently did that with our own website and pamphlets, we realized that we had been too "clubby" in what we said. The following are signs that you're inadvertently saying "join our club":

- You emphasize community and friendship more than spiritual depth or personal growth.

- You lead with your history, naming historical figures and events that non-members have a hard time relating to.
- You lead with lingo that only club members understand, such as "RE," "pastoral care," or "contact Jim" (with no contact information given).
- You make many assumptions about what people know. Some congregational websites fail to mention that they're LGBTQ-welcoming or wheelchair-accessible or that their children's program changes dramatically in the summer. Others don't list upcoming events, assuming that since they were listed in the congregational newsletter, the word has gotten out.
- You say "all are welcome," yet you don't give enough information about the experience you're promising in order for people to feel welcome and at ease.

If we had a dollar for every time we've heard a congregation say, "all are welcome" (including UU, UCC, Catholic, and even conservative evangelical), well, we'd have a lot of dollars. In being welcoming, we're not turning people away, but what are we actually offering? "All are welcome" at the movie theater, but we're still not going to the movies unless we know what's playing.

The key to successful outreach in the changing religious landscape, particularly with the unaffiliated or those who are spiritual but not religious, will likely be to address the issue of why people would want to show up in the first place, not just what can keep them there year after year. Describe what we offer for learning, yearning, and working for our values. We can't assume people are already looking for a church on Sunday mornings, because in fact we're competing for their time and attention with sleeping in, talking a walk, soccer practice, Facebook, and brunch. We have to focus on what we *do* as Unitarian Universalists, not just who we are.

How You Say It

How do we start talking like a "cause" and not a "club"? First, we do the heart work of lovingly holding two different perspectives: that of an outsider and that of an insider. Let's examine your perspective and how to upcycle it into some clear ways to invite people to engage with your congregation. Remember, a cause is an expression of something a person identifies with on a core level. A cause is action oriented, working to create change within us and/or beyond us. With that in mind, consider these questions:

- What causes do we work on collectively in our congregation?
- Are there individual opportunities (beyond our collective causes) that can draw someone into faithful relationship with our congregation?
- How could our congregation describe the *why* and the *what*, rather than just the *who* in the way we talk about ourselves?

Sarah, co-author of this essay, describes her experience:

I led a discussion about this with members of Follen Church in Lexington, Massachusetts, which I attended. Community had traditionally been strongly emphasized in the way the congregation talked about who it is and what it offers. Through this discussion, however, members got talking more deeply about many of the things that community had been shorthand for, about the causes at the heart of the congregation. These included:

- Affirming and encouraging us on diverse spiritual paths, through worship and meaningful programs for all ages.

- Recognizing and affirming young people for who they are, while supporting their growth in compassion, self-confidence, resilience, and wisdom.
- Learning to listen deeply, speak from the heart, and think with one another about important matters in Covenant Groups—small groups of adults that meet once a month, helping us live lives of integrity and interconnection.
- Cultivating wonder and beauty through music, with choirs and musical theater for children, youth, and adults and moving musical performances each week.
- Feeling hope in the face of despair; receiving spiritual nourishment to resist isolation, fear, and polarization.
- Forging connections across generations, races, cultures, abilities, identities, and creeds.
- Every week, helping us notice the ways we can make a difference in our own lives and in the world.
- Giving us ways to engage and make the world a better place, joining with movements like Black Lives Matter, climate justice, restorative justice, LGBTQ equality, immigration justice, and more.
- Creating meaningful, personalized rituals that surround the milestones of life with love, from birth to death.

These causes resonate with the people already in the congregation. The most compelling ones overlap with the causes embraced by those who are not yet in relationship with our congregation.

Being able to articulate what you do as a cause that others can join makes it far more accessible to people outside your community. You can tune your *offerings* to specific causes that people are ready to join.

What You Offer

As fewer Americans seek out religious communities, our congregations cannot wait for people to find them as they may have in the past. Inviting people in your area to connect with your congregation through specifically tailored offerings is a low-cost, high-impact way to introduce yourself to new people and audiences. You can also upcycle the energy you're putting into programming to create new entry points into the life of your congregation.

The two of us, Sarah and Carey, are now and for years have been deeply involved with congregations. We know how much pressure there can be to add more members, or grow more "pledge units." It can lead us to think in binary ways, dividing the people in relationship with the congregation into "pledgers" and "nonpledgers," or "members" and "nonmembers," those who count and those who don't. In collaboration with the Association of UU Membership Professionals, we've developed a way of thinking about the spectrum of faithful relationship. This helps us get away from the member/nonmember binary and embrace a more robust, healthy view of involvement in congregational life. A healthy congregation recognizes the important role of people all across a spectrum of faithful relationship, from the curious person who "likes" your page on Facebook to the deeply committed person who's serving her second term as chair of the board.

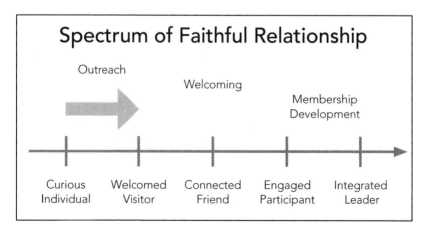

Spectrum of Faithful Relationship

Outreach
Welcoming
Membership Development

Curious Individual | Welcomed Visitor | Connected Friend | Engaged Participant | Integrated Leader

People move along the spectrum, sometimes slowly, sometimes quickly. A healthy and vibrant congregation respects the curious and the welcomed, creating opportunities for them to become connected, engaged, and integrated as they feel moved. And while membership growth is not the only metric for success, it is one important sign of a healthy church. Indeed, we see through surveys from the research group Faith Communities Today that having an outward-facing congregation is actually correlated with spiritual vitality, activism, and impact in the community.

Using the language of the spectrum of faithful relationship, "join our cause" events are the invitation to go from "curious individual" to "welcomed visitor." You begin by designing programs and events based on the personal causes of the people you want to reach: an event that addresses needs and desires they already know they have.

Many of us naturally think of Sunday morning services as such an event, because we know it speaks to our own causes. But curious folks don't often share that understanding, especially if they're not experienced churchgoers. Sunday morning is also a challenging time to make connections with people, especially if you're trying to chat with a greeter and juggle a cup of coffee while your children are tugging at your pant leg, or if you're just kind of shy.

Community events, programs, and gatherings are a more informal, easier way for visitors to get to know people in your congregation. The events that most effectively engage your participants will connect closely to your congregation's core sense of mission and an important cause in your community. This overlap of your strength and your community's need is your sweet spot. It is where you're most likely to tap into the energy and vitality that will make your congregation a success.

The Washington Ethical Society (WES) in Washington, D.C., knows about tailoring traditionally religious spaces to new audiences, especially for people who don't have much church experience. Its workshop series for parents on raising nonbelievers, building traditions in a nontraditional family, and prepping for deep talks on death and sex helped introduce its congregation to a new set of families. Advertised online and through social media, these workshops had about one-third nonmembers from the wider community. The promotion itself garnered one hundred new likes for its Facebook page from people who saw the events and wanted to learn more. "We've gotten in the habit of doing word-of-mouth outreach," says Teen Coordinator Robyn Kravitz. "When someone asks, we say, 'Here's my community, here's why it's great for me, I recommend you give it a try.'" By creating opportunities that really embody the congregation's sense of purpose as a way to connect with visitors, and by relentlessly getting the word out, WES is attracting more people who want to be a part of its mission and ministry.

Consider pursuing causes that are authentic to who you are and accessible to the people you're trying to reach. Embrace those activities that will truly knit your congregation together, and then create multiple pathways for those who share those causes to join with you. You'll know you have a great entry-point opportunity when it passes the "friend test"—you would be excited to invite your nonreligious friend to participate.

Whether you were born into Unitarian Universalism or found it after decades of life, we hope you will continue to choose it again and again because it resonates with who you are and what you care about most deeply. Upcycling our congregations from social club to mission hub, alive with purpose and possibility, is how we will reimagine our religious tradition for our time. May the *cause* of Unitarian Universalism flourish as we embrace the changing times and let the spirit of our congregations come alive in new and inspiring ways.

About the Contributors

Ken Beldon is the founding minister of WellSprings Congregation, located near Philadelphia, Pennsylvania. He is an editor and contributing author of *Restored to Sanity: Essays on the Twelve Steps by Unitarian Universalists* and *Wrestling with Adulthood: Unitarian Universalist Men Talking About Growing Up*, both published by Skinner House Books. In long-term recovery, he is currently pursuing a master's degree in social work.

Seth Fisher is the minister of First Unitarian Universalist Fellowship of Hunterdon County, New Jersey. In 2015 and 2016 he participated in the joint UUA/UUMA program, Beyond the Call: Entrepreneurial Ministry.

Julica Hermann de la Fuente is a lay community minister and a candidate for Unitarian Universalist ministry. She serves as a retreat leader for the Beloved Conversations program at Meadville Lombard's Fahs Collaborative and as a program leader for the UU College of Social Justice. She brings her experience as a social worker, master life coach, and social justice educator to the enterprise of helping Unitarian Universalists in their anti-racism work.

Sarah Lammert has served congregations in California, Utah, and New Jersey, and currently serves at the UUA as the co-director of Ministries and Faith Development, along with her colleague Jessica York. She believes that Unitarian Universalism has transforming power to share with a world in need.

Carey McDonald is the UUA's acting chief operating officer. He previously served as the UUA outreach director and the director of youth and young adult ministries. He is also a former lay member of the UUA Ministerial Fellowship Committee and the Skinner House Books Editorial Board. He lives in Medford, Massachusetts, with his wife, Sarah, and two sons, Julian and Hosea.

Christana Wille McKnight is the minister at First Parish Church in Taunton, Massachusetts. Previously, she had worked in other congregations and spent five years as a hospice and long-term care chaplain. She has served as president of the Ballou Channing Ministers' Association and as a trustee for the UUMA Board of Trustees. She lives in Seekonk, Massachusetts, with her husband, Eric, and their two children, Bryson and Deliah.

Sarah Gibb Millspaugh is a Unitarian Universalist minister currently serving congregations in the Pacific Western Region. She's worked on the UUA's Outreach Team, served as a parish minister, and developed multiple religious education curricula for youth and adults.

Donald Milton III is the full-time director of music at the Unitarian Universalist Congregation of Atlanta, the largest UU congregation in the Southeast. At UUCA, he runs one of the most eclectic and exceptional music programs in Atlanta. He's also an active choral conductor, clinician, performer, and arts advocate.

Elizabeth Norton serves First Parish in Concord, Massachusetts, as the director of music ministry. A UUA-credentialed music leader, she has served as president of the UU Musicians Network and on the UUA Council for Cross Cultural Engagement. She has composed several choral anthems and hymns and led UU singers on concert pilgrimages to Eastern Europe, building musical bridges with Unitarians in Romania, Hungary, and the Czech Republic.

Lee Paczulla is the executive minister at the WellSprings Congregation in Chester Springs, Pennsylvania. She began serving WellSprings as its ministerial intern in 2013, drawn to its fresh vision for what the future of spiritual community in our tradition might look like. Raised non-religious, she began her path to ministry in her twenties at All Souls Church, Unitarian in Washington, D.C.

Tandy Scheffler is the minister of faith formation and a credentialed religious educator, master level, at the Oak Ridge Unitarian Universalist Church in Oak Ridge, Tennessee. She is a former chairperson of the UUA's Religious Education Credentialing Committee. She currently serves as president of the Oak Ridge Ministers Association, an interfaith group that supports the common good of all city residents.

Vanessa Rush Southern is the senior minister at the First Unitarian Universalist Society of San Francisco. She has served churches in Boston, Massachusetts, Washington, D.C., and Summit, New Jersey. She is the author of *This Piece of Eden* and *Miles of Dream*, both published by Skinner House Books, and her writing has also appeared in *The Dallas Morning News*, *Scroll.in*, and *Woman's Day*.